The God Who Speaks

The God Who Speaks

LEARNING THE LANGUAGE OF GOD

Ben Campbell Johnson

WILLIAM B. EERDMANS PUBLISHING COMPANY
GRAND RAPIDS, MICHIGAN / CAMBRIDGE, U.K.

Wm. B. Eerdmans Publishing Co.
2140 Oak Industrial Drive N.E., Grand Rapids, Michigan 49505 /
P.O. Box 163, Cambridge CB3 9PU U.K.
www.eerdmans.com

Printed in the United States of America

09 08 07 06 05 04   7 6 5 4 3 2 1

Library of Congress Cataloging-in-Publication Data

Johnson, Ben Campbell.
The God who speaks: learning the language of God /
Ben Campbell Johnson.
p.   cm.
Includes bibliographical references.
ISBN 978-0-8028-2754-8 (pbk.: alk. paper)
1. Word of God (Theology) — History of doctrines. 2. Direct discourse in the Bible.
3. Language and languages — Religious aspects — Christianity. 4. Speech acts
(Linguistics) — Religious aspects — Christianity.   I. Title.

BT180.W67J64   2004
231.7′4 — dc22

2004040935

Contents

To

Dr. Tomas Scovel,

professor, linguist, missionary,

faithful disciple, gracious man,

and treasured friend

Introduction

More than five years ago I felt strongly guided to write on the subject of "the language of God." I began to think about the subject, to read in the field of linguistics, and to reflect on my own experiences to discover what the language of God is. Early on I intended to write a short devotional tract that would help women and men discern the voice of God in their experiences, both individually and as members of congregations.

About the time that I began musing over this issue, a number of books on discernment began to appear. Some of them dealt with personal spiritual guidance, others with spiritual guidance for congregations. I read these with delight and hoped that many would adopt the insights shared, because doing so would bring people into a deeper relationship with God. In my own writing I began to focus my interest more specifically on issues of God's speech. If we are to live before God, how does God speak to us, and how do we "hear" the voice of God?

The speech of God precedes all the issues of discernment. If we do not know that God is speaking to us, we need no discernment. What would we be discerning? So I began to think and pray about God's initiative in communicating Godself to us. How does God speak to us? In what ways does God reveal Godself to us? God's words and God's actions combine to manifest the nature and intent of God to us. What are these ways of speech?

Introduction

The contemporary church so often lacks an awareness of the divine presence in its midst, and this deficiency spurred me on in my search. Many faithful members of congregations hunger for a personal, meaningful relationship with God, and they often feel frustrated in their yearning. Even many deeply sincere elders and deacons in the church have not found a personal relationship with God. Often I hear them crying out for help. At the same time, many churches are just beginning to ask questions about the ways of God's Spirit and the possibility of transformative experiences of the divine presence.

Since the notion of God's calling and humans answering stands at the heart of all vital religion, and especially of Christianity, to ignore the voice of God cuts the nerve of transformative faith. An individual's spiritual life depends upon the "I" meeting the "Thou," in Martin Buber's phrase, and the communal life of the congregation relies equally upon the presence of God's speech in worship and mission. The loss of the conviction that God spoke in the past and still speaks today has dire consequences.

In the pages that follow, I will give testimony to "the God who speaks." In the first three sections of the book, I will set forth the biblical foundation of GodSpeech, the historical development of GodSpeech, and the practical applications of GodSpeech. In the fourth and final section I will explore some experiences of GodSpeech.

My hope is that this book will be used in classes for church leaders and by other interested individuals in the congregation. To this end I have provided questions for reflection and discussion at the end of each chapter, as well as ideas for keeping a journal as one moves through the chapters.

May we in the twenty-first-century church all come to know the God who speaks.

BEN JOHNSON

The Biblical Foundation

CHAPTER ONE

The God Who Speaks

The voice of the LORD is powerful; the voice of the LORD is full of majesty. The voice of the LORD breaks the cedars; the LORD breaks the cedars of Lebanon. He makes Lebanon skip like a calf, and Sirion like a young wild ox.

Psalm 29:4-6

The Story of Abram

Once upon a time there was a man of wealth, prestige, and deep sensitivity, but he was also a restless, searching, dissatisfied man. Daily when he counted his cattle and sheep and camels and the number of his servants and wives, he felt a mild satisfaction with his success, but still he felt a yearning in his soul for something he did not possess. Day and night this yearning possessed him. It invaded his every waking thought; it disrupted his meals and distracted him from fully participating in jubilant celebrations; it troubled his sleep. He could find no escape from this inner stirring, and because of this he chided himself: he should rejoice in all that he possessed. Yet his spirit remained dry and joyless. And the man's name was Abram.

Long ago, decades and centuries past, there was a man captured by wondering; his mind was always searching, questing. Although he had a wealth of possessions and commanded respect from his peers and his family, thoughts of an empty future undermined his hope. He concerned himself not with food to eat or wine to drink, but with name and place. Would he be without a son to carry on his name, and would his people always be without a land? Too soon he would grow old and die, and because he had no son to bear his name or extend his line, he feared that he would be forgotten and none would remember his name. He loved his wife, but she had been barren all these years. And now she was old in years, and he was too old to help her conceive. And the man's name was Abram.

In a distant land there lived a devout man who had seen thousands of sunsets and had awaited an equal number of sunrises. Daily he went to the altar to worship the gods. Regularly he made a sacrifice to atone for his sins. Those who knew him considered him a righteous man who lived faithfully. His wives and his servants respected him, and his brother and his nephew held him in high esteem. From time to time, deep within his soul, there arose intuitions of being special. He sometimes wondered if he were being chosen for a role he could not express or for a mission that he did not understand. He often wondered if he were destiny's child. Yet he had neither words nor images to describe these profound emotions that gripped him. But as surely as sunup follows sundown, his rising and retiring were fraught with a growing expectancy. Every day, as he worshipped faithfully before the smoking altar, he listened keenly for a word. His gods had mouths, but they did not speak. How desperately he longed to hear a word, a promise that would give him hope.

One morning Abram arose and washed his face and ate his curd with the feeling that it was a different kind of day. For reasons that he could not explain, this day seemed different from his days of yearning and years of wondering. On this day he did not spend time counting his cattle and sheep or numbering his servants; neither did he give place to

4

grieving his wife's barren womb. Although the years had prepared him for this day, he did not know that this was indeed destiny's day, a day that would be marked in his memory for as long as he lived. The moments passed slowly, like grains of sand falling through an hourglass. Late in the day, as the sun was dying a long, slow death, he heard a voice:

> "Go from your country and your kindred and your father's house to the land that I will show you. I will make of you a great nation, and I will bless you, and make your name great, so that you will be a blessing. I will bless those who bless you, and the one who curses you I will curse; and in you all the families of the earth shall be blessed." (Gen. 12:1-3)

And the man who did not understand the meaning of his yearning and did not comprehend the role of wonder became a man of destiny when the Voice spoke to him. This man heard the voice of God speak from the mystery that surrounded him. On hearing the Voice, he believed the promises.

The Voice and the words it spoke slaked his thirst, calmed his restlessness, and began to answer his wondering. The Voice spoke his name and promised him a place, a land that would belong to him and his descendants forever. The word echoed in his mind — *forever, forever, forever*. His name would endure. He would father a nation, a nation that would bless the world. He did not know how the promises would come to pass, but he trusted the Voice.

The man Abram so trusted the Voice that he set out toward the land promised him. Because he was an honorable and trustworthy man, his wives and his brother and his servants believed Abram's witness that God had spoken to him. Not only did he tell all of them about God's speaking to him, but in time he would also tell his yet-unborn sons, and they would tell their sons and daughters about the God who spoke to Abram. And the telling and retelling of the story of the Voice would sustain a nation that was destined to bless the world.

GodSpeech: A Definition

The story of Abram points to the most vital element in monotheistic religion, especially that form embodied in the Judeo-Christian tradition. This narrative asserts clearly and simply that God spoke to him: "Now the LORD said to Abram . . ." This brief phrase and the explication that follows reveal the most basic truth of Hebrew and Christian faith: God speaks to men and women, and they recognize God's voice and respond to it.

To be the recipient of the address of God implies that God knows the person being addressed. What can be more calming and reassuring to us than being known by God, and known deeply enough to be addressed? And this address suggests that God cares for us, that he considers us, like Abram, to be of great consequence. To be spoken to by God means not only that God knows us but also that God cares for us and expresses Godself to us. And nothing so characterizes us human beings as the need to be intimately related to the Creator and Sustainer of all things.

We do a disservice to God, to Abram, and to our faith when we place Abram in a special category as a hearer of God's voice. Isn't that true? We think that perhaps God spoke to Abram, the father of Israel, but we aren't certain that God speaks to us. Although some theologians have rejected the idea that God speaks in today's world, I choose to believe that God still speaks because nothing in the biblical revelation indicates that God has ceased speaking or has lost interest in speaking to us. Furthermore, scores of people testify that God has actually spoken to them.

Likewise, we commit the same error when we imagine that God spoke to Abram in those distant biblical times and then withdrew into silence. This kind of thinking places the biblical narratives of divine experiences in a special category inaccessible to persons in the "modern" world. Why do we have confidence that God could speak to Abram but not to us?

Perhaps our segregating the experience of God's speech reported in Scripture from our own hearing of it has been fortified by false images.

In the case of Abram, we imagine the Voice speaking as if through a megaphone, shouting to Abram in Hebrew or Aramaic. But what if God did not shout at Abram but spoke in a flash or a gentle flow of thoughts into his mind? In some ways these were normal thoughts like he had had before, yet in other ways they were very different. These thoughts about a land, a nation, and being a blessing were ideas he had pondered in the same way he had pondered the number of his sheep, his cattle, and his servants. But, though similar in nature, these thoughts flowed into his mind effortlessly. The ideas were clear, sharp, and focused. In addition, Abram had the conviction that these words did not arise from within him but came to him. Something or Someone was speaking to him, engaging his mind, his thoughts, and his emotions, but at the same time it was much more than that.

This speech of God is not only a possibility — it is an imperative. It lies at the heart of vital faith and fullness of life. God speaking to humans and humans responding to God provides the matrix for life, for meaning and vocation. And, when the individual or the community turns away from the God who speaks, faith, life, and mission wane.

I have much to say about GodSpeech, by which I mean the disclosure of God to us. There are two kinds of GodSpeech: primary, which is God's direct speech to us or our direct speech to God; and secondary, which is our speech about God. Primary GodSpeech refers to all the ways that God addresses us and all our direct responses to God. Secondary GodSpeech refers to our speech about God, our efforts to conceptualize, define, proclaim, or give witness to our primary experiences of God. Secondary GodSpeech may become primary GodSpeech when God chooses to speak to others through our speech — as, for example, in preaching and in testimony.

God's speech to us may come through intuition and imagination, as I have described Abram's experience, or it may occur through things like sermons, faithful witnesses, and the concurrence of events in our lives. These and other means constitute God's way of speaking to us.

Yet, God's address through any of these means must finally be expressed in words. Even when the speech of God comes to us through intuition or through words spoken by human lips or through strange, providential happenings, it must be translated into words to be intelligible. Without words we may experience a vague awareness of the divine mystery, or a mystical fusion with the holy, or a pronounced interruption in our lives, but communication ultimately demands words — pure, simple, comprehensible words. The words that we use to express our experiences of God, whether through intuition or imagination, are part of what I mean by GodSpeech. GodSpeech, therefore, is the communication of Godself to human beings through a variety of media, communication that ultimately must take shape in words. The word of God makes God different from all so-called gods.

In particular, the God who speaks contrasts sharply with all the pagan gods of Abram's era and the substitute gods of every era. The psalmist clearly distinguishes between the God of Abram and all idols when he writes,

> Our God is in the heavens; he does whatever he pleases. Their idols are silver and gold, the work of human hands. They have mouths, but do not speak; eyes, but do not see. They have ears, but do not hear; noses, but do not smell. They have hands, but do not feel; feet, but do not walk; they make no sound in their throats. Those who make them are like them; so are all who trust in them. (Ps. 115:3-8)

Hebrew faith was born out of this speech to Abram, and that faith has been nurtured continuously by the divine voice. When followers of Abram cease to attend to the voice of God, the promises grow dull, and the sense of the divine presence diminishes. A deeper reflection on this divine speech will reveal its crucial role in both personal and communal life.

GodSpeech: Personal, Purposive, Persistent

So far as we know, only humans speak. Other animals communicate, but only humans have both the physical and the psychological capacities to speak. When, therefore, we say that the Lord spoke to Abram, we are asserting that God is personal. By this I do not mean that God is a person like you or me, but that God possesses all those capacities distinctive of persons — consciousness, knowledge, feelings, intuition, and freedom to choose and relate.

Even before the Voice spoke, God was present in the life of Abram. The man had been blessed with good fortune. But only when the Voice spoke to this wandering Aramean did he realize that God knew him. The awareness of the Voice speaking to him, calling his name, awakened him to the personal nature of the divine mystery that surrounded his life. And his life was enriched beyond measure.

Within a few centuries of Abram, the Sumerians, Egyptians, and Babylonians were worshipping a pantheon of gods, and at times acknowledged a "high god." But in the mythologies of these ancient religions, there was no deity who spoke and in that speech claimed to be the one, true, and only God. The God who spoke to Abram would later say to Moses, "I am the LORD your God, who brought you out of the land of Egypt, out of the house of slavery; you shall have no other gods before me" (Exod. 20:1-2).

God's speaking these words to Abram has profound significance for those who walk in the Judeo-Christian tradition. This divine utterance was not casual chatter, like a morning greeting or a passing inquiry; it was highly purposeful speech.

The divine communication was not only personal and purposive but also persistent. The God who spoke on that memorable day continued to speak to Abram during seasons of drought and plenty, during struggles with his people and with rulers, and during times when the promises seemed long in coming. God's continuous word to Abram inspired courage and kept hope alive even when the fulfillment of the promises seemed impossible.

This speech, like all speech, reveals aspects of the Speaker. The content of the promises to Abram suggests a gracious God, One who longs to give himself to humankind. What soul could hear the words "I will bless you," "I will make your name great," and "You will be a blessing," and not be overwhelmed with the graciousness of God?

9

This speech to Abram also created a relationship between him and God, and the continued speech clarified, strengthened, and enriched the relationship. A linguist friend tells me that speech is used primarily to initiate and maintain social relationships and secondarily to transfer information. In other words, conversation is primarily interpersonal, not transactional. Without meaningful speech, relationships fall into pits of misunderstanding, which lead to estrangement. The God who speaks opens doors of relatedness in all who hear.

Unfortunately, many of us have never learned to listen for this divine speech. And some would even raise serious questions about the affirmations made here.

Was There an Abram?

By retelling the narrative of Abram, I intend his experience of encountering God to serve as a model of God's speech to others — prophets, wise men, and you and me. For my purposes, I treat the story of Abram as a parable or metaphor with multiple symbolic implications for our lives and for the community of faith today. However, to choose Abram as a model poses certain difficulties, since some question Abram and his story on a number of levels. Did he truly exist? Was his God simply an illusion created out of humankind's wish for a father? Was Abram a megalomaniac who simply imagined that God spoke to him? All these objections are worthy of consideration.

Some Old Testament scholars claim that a person by the name of Abram never really existed. They suggest either that Abram represents a composite of leaders in Israel, or that Abram was a figment of the writer's imagination. Others would say that the Abram story provides a mythological explanation of Israel's origin. But I find no great difficulty in believing that a person similar to Abram — if not Abram himself — did live in centuries past, and that he was the recipient of God's words. And even if such an individual never existed, we are still confronted with a people who have believed the message God spoke to Abram. These people have been so convinced of the veracity of God's speech that they have endured for over three-and-a-half millennia. The belief that the One God spoke to Abram lies at the heart of this conviction and empowers these people in the most trying of circumstances.

Some objectors would say that the very idea of God speaking is but one more example of the anthropomorphism that contaminates religious faith. Claiming that God speaks, they would explain, belongs to the childhood of the race, but certainly not to modernity, not to "man come of age." To claim that God speaks to people, makes them promises, and fulfills these intentions simply verifies Freud's claim that God is an illusion, the mere projection of unconscious longings.

If, as the faithful believe, humans are made in the image of God, how could God not possess speech? If God speaks, the Word gives birth and life to all who hear. I choose not to be dissuaded by the anthropomorphic aspersion. How can we speak of God except by analogy? Analogy is the friendliest way — if not the only way — to speak of the Divine.

A Freudian interpretation of God's promises to Abram would also suggest that they reveal in Abram and thus in us the longing for approval and security from a father figure. And the yearning for greatness that all creatures experience is fulfilled in the promise that Abram will be great and the father of many nations. What could be more godlike than the ability to influence the whole world? But this is a psychological interpretation that does not recognize the reality of the Voice that spoke to Abram.

The history of human egoism and its godlike claims suggests that illusions of supermen or super-races tend to collapse. The insanity of Nietzsche and the godlike ambition of Hitler reveal the destructive side of this will to power or godlikeness. Nietzsche and Hitler were megalomaniacs undone by their illusions. By contrast, the word of God to Abram led Abram into periods of testing and sustained him through experiences of failure, eventually resulting in the establishment of a nation. And Christians believe that Abram realized God's promise in the birth of Jesus Christ, whose life and ministry have powerfully changed the world.

Others who are skeptical of GodSpeech will suggest that scriptural assertions that God spoke should be taken metaphorically. Describing

God as One who speaks to humans was a convenient way for the biblical writers to frame their vision of God. These literary critics would classify the references to God speaking as one genre of literature. But looking upon references to the speech of God as a particular type of writing does not preclude the possibility that God did in fact speak.

If God did not speak, what occurred to create a faith that has persisted for so many centuries? If someone does not wish to believe that a personal contact with God is a present possibility, a thousand cases for doubt can be created. I choose to be an enlightened believer who holds that the divine mystery did and does make itself known.

Finally, most scholars have pointed to the covenant as the genius of Israel's faith — not, as I urge, hearing promises from a God who speaks. Granted, the covenant is crucial in Israel's life, but how could there be a covenant between God and the nation without speech? Embracing the covenant does indeed provide a foundation for Israel's life. And the covenant of God reaches from the past to this very moment. But an exclusive focus on the covenant can turn our attention to the past, and constantly looking backward distracts us from listening to God today.

Like Israel, most of us today do not need to hear the Covenant reread; however, we do need to hear the God who speaks to us speak here and now. Despite the risks and the objections of some, the followers of Yahweh need to recover a posture of listening.

These brief responses to the issues raised about Abram may not provide you with sufficient grounds for claiming that God spoke to him. Indeed, I rather doubt that the case can be made scientifically that Abram heard God speak. But I think it is obvious that Israel believed that God did speak to Abram, and on the basis of this conviction they understood their identity and their destiny. And the existence of this people points to the issue that concerns me — faith in the God who speaks.

Probing the Word to Abram

As I have indicated, I chose Abram because he is an excellent model of the crucial implications of GodSpeech. I am persuaded that vital faith is born and nourished through a continuous encounter with this God who speaks.

Exactly how the Voice came to Abram we do not know. In *Mysticism*, Evelyn Underhill writes about the nature of what she calls "true auditions" and describes the characteristics that accompany them. She suggests that such a moment of hearing God comes when the mind is absorbed — that is, without conscious thought. It comes from the depths of the psyche in the form of a sudden and ungovernable uprush of knowledge. Often this inbreaking of a word or the Voice startles us with its abruptness. Yet we hear these words more clearly than if they had been spoken in our ear. They are "impossible not to understand," she says.[1] Perhaps Abram's experience was marked by these characteristics.

While numerous biblical characters could have been chosen to demonstrate GodSpeech, I chose Abram because his story offers clear and helpful guidelines for our learning the language of God.

Learning this language presents a challenge, but it also makes all the difference in our relationship. I recall the early days of my marriage to my wife, Nan, when I was feeling a bit uncared for, and I said to her, "Why don't you ever tell me that you love me?" (I, of course, was verbose and constantly told her how much I loved her and that I couldn't live without her. I may have *over*affirmed my affection.)

Rather than becoming defensive and bickering with me over the issue, Nan simply said, "When you come home, where am I?"

"You are always here," I answered.

Again, she asked, "And when you want to do something, how do I respond?"

"You nearly always support me and go along with my ideas."

"What do you think that means?" she asked me.

"That you love me and want to be with me," I responded with embarrassment.

"You see," she said, "I don't communicate in the same manner that you do."

1. Underhill, *Mysticism: A Study in the Nature and Development of Spiritual Consciousness* (New York: Doubleday, 1990), p. 275.

That brief encounter showed me how strongly I wanted her to change and speak in my language, but she had her own language that I needed to understand and honor. I had a choice: I could either learn her language and hear what her actions were saying, or I could be filled with self-pity and feel unloved and uncared for.

We have a similar choice with God. Either we can complain that God does not speak as we wish he did, or we can learn the manner in which God actually speaks. At this point Abram may be of some help to us. Let's review what we can learn from his encounter with God.

1. *God spoke to Abram out of divine initiative — Abram was not expecting it.* Perhaps if Abram had known more about the ways of GodSpeech, he would have recognized that his yearning and wondering and feeling dissatisfied were harbingers of GodSpeech, but he did not know God's ways. So we can surmise that he spent his days yearning and wondering but not expecting God to speak to him.

Abram's experience describes the experience of most of us. We have yearnings, hungers, and questions, but we are unaware that they express a deep longing for God. Only after accumulated experience do we begin to see that these movements in the heart are the forerunners to God's address of us. Perhaps we would benefit from reading our hearts and looking for signs of God's preparing us to hear a word.

2. *God spoke to an individual.* The promise came not to Abram's family but to Abram personally. In all likelihood, he immediately shared it with his wife, and doubtless he spoke to his father and his kin. GodSpeech was first personal, given to an individual, and then was communicated through this one person to the community.

God still speaks to people in community, but generally it is not a word heard by everyone in the community simultaneously. When God spoke to William Carey about taking the gospel to those who had never heard it, he spoke to the church community and persisted in speaking until the modern missionary movement was born.

In our day God spoke to Charles Colson through his prison experience, and he mobilized the church to undertake a mission to prisoners.

God speaks to one for the sake of the many, and the one who hears speaks to the many on behalf of God. When God speaks to us, usually it is not for our sake alone but for others as well.

3. *God's address to Abram included a call and a promise of assistance.* Abram was called to be the Father of Israel, the source of blessing to the nations. The task exceeded his ability, and only with divine assistance would he be able to fulfill the call.

Not every word spoken by God includes a call: some GodSpeech is about guidance, encouragement, hope, and consolation. But today the Spirit often issues calls. Women and men are called into ordained ministry through this speech, and countless laypersons are called into a ministry as well. All the baptized, of course, are called through their baptism into vocations. The definition of these callings often comes through a specific word from God — that is, a call to a specific ministry.

4. *God's word to Abram recognized him as a person.* Like all of us, he wondered what his life was about. Why was he born? What was he to do? How could he find meaning? All these issues were settled for him by the Voice that spoke and promised him purpose and blessing. This promise of God clarified his identity. He knew who he was and what he was to do.

This principle still applies today. Many who journey aimlessly through life, searching for a reason for being, find it in the call of God. Untold multitudes have seen themselves as directionless wanderers until God spoke to them and gave them a sense of identity and direction in their lives. Karl Barth put it clearly when he said, "In speaking to me God has chosen me, as the man I am, to be the man I am. The new quality I acquire through the Word of God is my true and essential quality. . . . I am wholly and altogether the man I am in virtue of the divine decision."[2]

5. *God's word left an indelible imprint upon Abram, one to which he could return again and again.* The evidence seems to point to the fact that Abram recalled this promise from God and told his sons, and they in

2. Barth, *Church Dogmatics*, I/1 (Edinburgh: T&T Clark, 1975), pp. 161-62.

turn told their sons. The promise of God was passed on from one person to another, and usually the person to whom the promise was passed received a word of confirmation. Think, for example, of Jacob, Abram's grandson, for whom the promise was confirmed at Bethel. And the confirmation came to Moses in the desert when the Voice spoke through the burning bush. These transcendent moments were recounted time and time again in the communal life of Israel.

The remembrance of a God-moment, a moment when you knew yourself to be in the presence of the Holy, brings renewed energy and power. At those points where God has touched our lives, there seems to be a sustained spiritual energy that, when we revisit it, empowers us. The recollection of such personal experiences is similar to visiting the Mount of Transfiguration or the Sea of Galilee, where Peter met the risen Lord. When you go there and recall what occurred there, you enter into that moment and often are imbued with the power of the Spirit. The watermark experiences in our lives seem to retain their transformative power through the years. The continued power of these recollected events hints at their divine origin.

A friend of mine named Phil wrote to me the other day about his experience of GodSpeech. He told me, "God has spoken to me a couple of times; not more than that. One time I was resisting the idea of going to seminary, and I wanted some miraculous sign, or undeniable charismatic gift — anything, really. Something to really cement my faith, I thought. I was praying, and the Spirit said to me, 'You will always have enough faith to believe, and never more than that. I'm sending you to reach a certain type of person, and I will make sure you have everything you need to be faithful. I'm not going to load you down with things you don't need, even if you want them.' I've had to be content with that."

This simple testimony gathers up all of the insights found in Abram's experience. God spoke to Phil when God chose to speak, and God issued an individual call to Phil that clarified, directed, and empowered his life. He was promised what he needed for his task. And time and again he has returned to that moment to renew his sense of the promise and the direction of his life.

QUESTIONS FOR REFLECTION AND DISCUSSION

1. How was God's speech at the core of Hebrew faith? What does this suggest about the faith?
2. What was the effect of God's speech to Abram? What changed?
3. What principles of discerning God's revelation appear in this story?
4. What is the most important insight for you in this chapter?

SUGGESTIONS FOR JOURNALING

1. Describe your thoughts about God's speaking to people today.
2. Sit quietly and consider your feelings about having God speak to you. Then write down your reflections.
3. Complete this sentence in two or three paragraphs: "I believe God spoke to me . . ."

CHAPTER TWO

GodSpeech in Christ

The voice of the LORD *is over the waters;*
the God of glory thunders,
the LORD, *over mighty waters.*

Psalm 29:3

God whispered to Abraham and spoke audibly to Moses, and in Jesus, God embodied Godself. Jesus, who is called Christ, makes God's Word visible and tangible in our midst. Abraham heard God's promise and became the head of a nation destined to bless the world. Moses heard God's promise and led the Israelites out of captivity. Christ enfleshed God's speech and became the Head of the church, his Body on earth. Jesus not only spoke the Word of God to people: he was in fact the Word of God. Jesus is the full content of God's speech; God spoke Jesus to the world.

Borrowing images from Greek philosophy, the early church had a profound way of making this claim. The prologue to the Gospel of John states it succinctly:

In the beginning was the Word, and the Word was with God, and the Word was God. He was in the beginning with God. All things came into being through him, and without him not one thing came into being. What has come into being in him was life, and the life was the light of all people. The light shines in the darkness, and the darkness did not overcome it. . . . And the Word became flesh and lived among us, and we have seen his glory, the glory as of a father's only son, full of grace and truth. . . . No one has ever seen God. It is God the only Son, who is close to the Father's heart, who has made him known. (John 1:1-5, 14, 18)

This sublime text makes audacious claims, claims that lie at the foundation of the Christian faith. The writer of the Fourth Gospel asserts that from the beginning the Word of God "was." This goes beyond Christ's merely being with God or in God: "the Word was God." This relationship of Father and Son, between God and the Word, existed since the beginning. This claim means that what we meet in Jesus of Nazareth did not have its beginning with Jesus' advent on earth. This Word of God — that is, the self-expression of God — always existed.

The Word of God, the Logos, served as the agent of creation — "all things came into being through him." He had the power to form what had never been, to change nonbeing into being, to change nothing into something. In the process of creation through this agency of the Word, Christ's fingerprints marked every created thing. Nothing he created is alien to him; everything has the potential of communicating with him or being acted upon by him.

The life that came forth on the earth came through him; his light shone in all the creatures to which he gave life. And this light of God shining through the creation also shines in the hearts and souls of men and women. Despite the darkness of the world and the dimmed eyes of human understanding, this light has not been and cannot be extinguished. This light keeps flashing signals, illuminating the pathway, giving humans enough vision to stumble along until they come into the fullness of light.

This astounding witness to Jesus asserts, "And the Word became flesh and lived among us, and we have seen his glory, the glory as of a father's only son, full of grace and truth." Ponder this amazing truth. The God who has always existed came among us, clothed in human flesh, to speak to us. He who was and is the Word of God spoke the Word of God so that we might hear the Word of God and see it too (1 John 1:1-2). Who he was and what he did constitute the speech of God.

Jesus' Life and Ministry as the Parable of God

Because Jesus is God's Word made visible and tangible, I invite you to think of him as "the parable of God." By extending this invitation I am not rejecting the historical dimension of Jesus' birth, life, ministry, death, and resurrection. I am simply inviting you to look at Jesus from a particular perspective, to look at the speech of God to humanity in the form of a parable. This perspective opens up the Jesus event in new ways that can help us hear and understand the speech of God today.

Key elements make "parable" a helpful way to look at Jesus of Nazareth: the narrative character of parable, and its metaphor-like potential for evoking additional dimensions of insight. The story form helps us visualize as well as hear the meaning intended. The parable constitutes a contextualized mode of speech because to be effective it must grow out of the values and worldview of the hearers. So the parable generally addresses a culture's values and aims. Like the prophets before him, Jesus used the parable to draw people into the unfolding truth of its narrative.

A parable proves effective because it has multiple meanings; a parable can never be exhausted by a single interpretation. Furthermore, the meaning of a parable is affected by what a listener hears and sees in it. The listener's worldview, mode of consciousness, and motives shape what he or she hears.

The parable, while challenging us with new insights, also makes room for us to be human. Being human in this sense does not imply being self-centered or self-willed, but instead suggests a full humanity drawing upon the image of God within us.

Finally, the parable is inexhaustible. No matter how many times it is heard, a fresh meaning always emerges because of the constant changes in the hearer and the hearer's world.

Jesus' parable of the sower and the three kinds of soil illustrates these points. First, it is a narrative with a rural context that helps us grasp its meaning through the images it presents. What we take from it can depend on whether we focus on the sower or the soil. Some of us see ourselves as one of the kinds of soil: wayside soil, weedy soil, or good soil. Others of us focus on the actions of the sower. Our perspective depends upon whether we identify with the sower or with the soil.[1] The life experience and the maturity that each of us brings to the story further shape the perspective — that is, what we bring to the story influences how we hear it. Very gently the story draws us into its message. These different types of soil indicate the frailty of human nature, but the narrative leaves room for us to be fully human. Finally, this story is inexhaustible because it points to enduring issues in human life and it addresses us in our different stages of personal and spiritual development.

As we look at Jesus' life and ministry as the parable of God, these multidimensional aspects of the meaning of parable will assist us in hearing God's Word to us in Christ and help explain how we hear such diverse messages in Christ.

Jesus' Life and Ministry as GodSpeech

Since Jesus is the Word of God in parable form, looking at each aspect of Jesus' life and ministry provides clues that will enable us, with a bit of reflection, to better understand God's language. As important as Jesus being "God in the flesh" may have been, this visible, tangible communication of God still required words. The revelation of God could not be reduced to words; at the same time, it was not complete without words. To know what God says to humanity, we must look at Jesus. In him God

1. A friend of mine first gained this insight when she was listening to a sermon on this parable by Allan Boesak. Since she had not grown up in an agrarian society, she had always heard this as the parable of the soils — a lesson on how receptive we are to hearing the voice of God. Allan helped her to see that in a society where seed is as valuable as currency, no sower would ever sow seed on soil that would not allow it to take root. So from his perspective, this was the parable of the sower, whose grace was so abundant that it did not concern itself with where the seed fell. This really opened my eyes!

"spoke" a person, a parable of truth, and God came as near humanness as possible. In the language of Incarnation, God spoke the clearest and most powerful speech anyone can speak. Because of the profundity of this speech, our task will be to explore who Jesus was and what he did with enough imaginative depth to find clues to the recognition of GodSpeech today. For our purposes we will look for these clues in the angel's announcement, Jesus' birth, his baptism, his testing, his ministry, and his death and resurrection.

The Announcement

The story of this living parable begins with a rehearsal of Jesus' genealogy connecting him with Abraham, who had received the promise years before. Matthew declares: "An account of the genealogy of Jesus the Messiah, the son of David, the son of Abraham" (Matt. 1:1). The events that unfolded fulfilled the promise made centuries before to that wandering Aramean, the Father of Faith. At the time appointed, a messenger of God appeared to Joseph, a man engaged to Mary, a young woman who was "with child." The angel told him not to be afraid to marry her because the child was from the Holy Spirit (Matt. 1:20). According to Matthew's perception, these events took place to fulfill this all-important prophecy: "Look, the virgin shall conceive and bear a son, and they shall name him Emmanuel," which means, 'God is with us'" (Matt. 1:21-22).

What does this announcement of Jesus' birth show us about the ways of GodSpeech? First of all, it shows us that God is faithful to promises made. God's promise to bless the world through Abraham found fulfillment in Jesus of Nazareth. Thus we can depend upon what God promises, even if it is long in coming.

Promised years before, the appearance of God's messenger took Mary by surprise. She was a young woman, probably in her teens, and this heavenly being suddenly appeared, announcing that she had been chosen by God to bear a son through the Holy Spirit. This news shocked her — thus the angel's admonition, "Fear not." This shows us that surprise and anxiety often accompany GodSpeech. Aren't you shocked when God addresses you? You ask, "Why did you speak at this time? Why did you speak to me?" Like Mary, we find that this Word of God startles us out of our accustomed way of seeing our futures and ourselves.

The announcement to Mary also contradicts human wisdom and expectation. Who would have imagined that the Word of God would come to an unheard-of young woman in an obscure village? And who would ever have imagined that the God of Abraham would appear in human flesh! Yet this is precisely what happened: "the word became flesh."

God's word often creates confusion, just as it befuddled Mary. God's direction may also break with social custom: in Mary's case, she became pregnant before she was married. This God who breaks up old arrangements of long-established social values often begins this transformation by addressing one person. This dialect of GodSpeech not only addresses an individual but also speaks to a community through the individual, creating radical change.

All these contradictions of human ways characterize the way of God. The Creator God did not appear as an emperor or a king, with a fanfare of trumpets, with splendor and power. No — he appeared as a baby. How different from human aspirations! Ambitious men and women assert themselves to get attention or wield power. Humans generally are vocal, pretentious, and self-centered, but God's speech in Christ utterly contradicts this way.

God's speech may contradict human wisdom, but it remains consistent with God's past ways. This announcement confirms God's earlier promise to bless the world. The coming of God in the flesh into history expresses the divine intention to be ever closer to humankind. In a section of *Church Dogmatics* entitled "The Word of God as the Speech of God," Karl Barth alludes to F. C. Oetinger's statement that "corporeality is the end of all the ways of God."[2] God first chose a person, and through this person chose a nation, and from that nation chose a woman in whom to become flesh — a consistent unfolding achieving "the end of all the ways of God."

---

2. Barth, *Church Dogmatics,* I/1 (Edinburgh: T&T Clark, 1975), p. 134.

These principles of surprise, contradiction, and consistency provide the nuances of GodSpeech.

The Birth

Joseph, a faithful man, embraced a pregnant young woman as his wife. When she was ready to deliver the child, the young couple traveled from Galilee to Bethlehem to register in the Roman census. While they were there, Mary delivered her son. Wise men, astrologers from Persia, came to pay homage to the child — but did not know where to find him. Traveling to Jerusalem, they asked King Herod where the Messiah had been born. According to their testimony, they had seen GodSpeech in the stars: "we observed his star at its rising" (Matt. 2:2). After Herod had inquired of the chief priests and scribes, he told the Wise Men that the prophecy said that Christ would be born in Bethlehem. He sent them there, requesting that they notify him when they found the child. But the Wise Men, after finding the child and offering him their gifts, proceeded on their way home, having been warned about Herod in a dream sent from God. Filled with anger and paranoia, Herod slaughtered all the male children of Bethlehem who were two years old or younger.

The report of Christ's birth shows us several amazing aspects of the ways of GodSpeech. First of all, God speaks to people outside the Hebrew tradition in ways that they understand and act upon. The Wise Men, trained in astrology, saw God's speech through the configuration of stars. They followed Christ's star, traveling to Judah and stopping in Jerusalem to inquire where the Christ-child was. Their question proved to be an announcement to Herod and the chief priests and scribes of Jesus' birth. The visit of the Wise Men suggests that GodSpeech is not limited to the Jewish or Christian tradition. God speaks to those beyond the boundaries of this unique history.

Further, the visit of the Wise Men also suggests that those outside the tradition may speak God's word to the tradition, as the Magi, through Herod, spoke to the chief priests and scribes. Is it possible that God is speaking to the Christian tradition through Muhammadanism, the New Age movement, or even secular humanism? Have others seen truths that we have missed, or have they engaged parts of our tradition that we have lost?

Finally, we see clearly that speaking about God to the "powers" — political, military, or economic — often evokes rage. The Wise Men spoke about God's revelation, and in his fury Herod slew all the young male children in Bethlehem.

The Baptism

God's approving speech provides the climax of Jesus' baptism. When Jesus came up out of the water, God's voice declared, "This is my Son, the Beloved, with whom I am well pleased" (Matt. 3:17). This approving word from God clarified Jesus' identity and verified his mission. Perhaps his sense of identity had been emerging during those mysterious years when he worked as a carpenter, attended synagogue, and memorized psalms. But the confirmation of his identity came in a charismatic moment when the Holy Spirit descended upon him and the Voice spoke from heaven. This was the same Voice that had spoken to Abraham at the birth of the nation Israel.

God's speech confirms our identity and our mission. Joined to a sacrament of the church like baptism, GodSpeech appears much clearer. I recall one woman telling me about the first time she attended church. "The minister spoke only to me," she said. And when she was baptized, she heard Christ's words of affirmation to her: "You are my daughter." GodSpeech confirms our personhood, just as it confirmed that of Abraham and Jesus.

If Jesus is the Speech of God to us, what is God saying through the baptismal event? I believe that when he said to Jesus, "This is my Son, the Beloved, with whom I am well pleased," God was at the same time speaking an affirmation to the human family. All humanity was present in Jesus at the baptism, and all were thus affirmed in him. Such speech comes to us in the minister's words during the ritual of baptism: "I baptize you in the name of the Father, the Son, and the Holy Spirit." And the baptismal water becomes a visible, sensory confirmation of the spoken words of inclusion in Christ. (Notice how the implications of Christ's baptism can also be found in the announcement to Mary.)

The Testing

The affirmation of Jesus' personhood at his baptism did not go without testing. Was he truly the Son of God? Immediately after the baptism, the Spirit led Jesus into the desert. The desert meant enduring a period of self-denial and testing and thus discovering his call. In the desert Jesus found the place of transformation, a conversion that came through prayer and fasting. When he completed the fast, "the tempter" said to him, "If you are the Son of God, command these stones to become loaves of bread" (Matt. 4:3). This and each of the other suggestions the devil made challenged his confidence in his identity as the Son of God. In each instance Jesus remained faithful to God's affirmation. He withstood every temptation and insinuation of the Evil One.

God's affirmative word to us undergoes the same kind of testing; often it comes in the form of doubt. The tempter says, "Is this really God who has spoken to you? If you are called by God, prove it by accomplishing extraordinary feats." When God has spoken to us, we should expect to be tested.

At one stage in writing about "the God who speaks," I was engulfed by doubt. I began wondering if I truly believed that God speaks to us, and if so, was I the person to write about it? This struggle lasted for the better part of a month, and during that period I couldn't write a word. One morning it occurred to me to re-read the first GodSpeech that I had heard and written down, which I called "First Words" (included later in the "Experiences of Intensive Listening" section). This is what I read:

I AM the God who speaks; above all else, I speak to my people and show myself to them. Do not be anxious, my son. I have chosen to come to you and speak to you. The idea of GodSpeech that came

26

into your mind years ago was not of your own making. I approached you under the cover of thought and in the hiddenness of your intuition so that you would receive my guidance in the most unobtrusive way. . . .

I know you. You cannot do this task you have set for yourself, but I can. I can show myself to you and help you shape the words that grasp the vision. I can speak in your ear and translate the words in your heart. Yes, I am your God, and I choose to speak to you.

I have known you from all eternity, and I have known this moment would come from the day that you were conceived in my mind and from the day that you were conceived in your mother's womb. None of those who saw your birth would ever have suspected the intent I had for you. Even now, if they were standing before you, they would have trouble believing what I am about to do.

Do not be anxious about me; do not be anxious about others and what you imagine they are saying and thinking. It is enough for you to listen. Listen to me and write what I tell you so that it may build up my people in a time when they have ceased to believe that I speak. I will come to them and take them by the hand and lead them on the pathway of my intention and their fulfillment.

As my own experience indicates, the affirmative speech of God does not go untested. But when it is tested, it becomes strong, durable, and ultimately dependable.

The Ministry

In the account of Jesus' life, the time from his birth to his baptism is a nearly blank slate, marked only by a brief account of his attending a festival in Jerusalem. This is not all that surprising, since the ministry of Jesus begins at the time of his baptism. How do we view him and his ministry as a Word from God? Since it is my purpose to be illustrative and not exhaustive, I will briefly examine his being, doing, and speaking. This will give us great insight into his ministry.

The language spoken in Jesus comes first of all through his being, who he was — not his doing and not his speaking. The angel announced the enfleshment of the divine in the human: "the Word became flesh and lived among us." At the baptism the Voice affirmed his identity: "You are my much-loved Son." God spoke in Jesus' ordinary, daily life. Those who encountered him saw in him or through him visions of the divine.

Jesus came very close to acknowledging this when he said to the Jews, "Before Abraham was, I am" (John 8:58). Jesus existed before the days of Abraham, and his use of the "I am" phrase has overtones of God's response to Moses when he requested the divine name: "I AM has sent me to you" (Exod. 3:14).

In another incident, Jesus went into the synagogue on the Sabbath. As he was teaching those assembled, a man who was possessed by an evil spirit cried out, "What have you to do with us, Jesus of Nazareth? Have you come to destroy us? I know who you are, the Holy One of God" (Mark 1:24). The demoniac seemed to be in touch with the spiritual dimension, albeit in a negative way, and he recognized Jesus. The very nature of Christ communicated with him before Jesus spoke or cast out his demon.

In this instance the communication of God through the being of Christ got translated into words: "I know who you are, the Holy One of God." God spoke through the transparency of Jesus' being, and God permitted the split personality in the synagogue to identify him. In Jesus, God spoke the language of Incarnation, the clearest and most dramatic speech the world has seen.

The "being of Christ" as a communication of God to us strongly suggests that his presence in other persons also speaks God to us today. Let's think for a moment. Haven't we all met individuals or known people who radiated the message of God? When we are with this kind of person, it is not what they say about God but who they are in God that becomes unspoken but clearly communicated GodSpeech. Perhaps later, after our encounter with them, we recall how the Spirit of God flowed through their lives. In this way we experience GodSpeech without words, though afterward we translate the meeting into words.

What is the Word of God in the actions of Jesus? When he calls people to follow him, is he not asserting the inclusive nature of God's partnership with us? When he feeds the hungry, does he not articulate God's desire that basic human needs be met? When he heals the infirm or the emotionally disturbed, does this not communicate God's will for the wholeness of persons? Reading the actions of God in this way enables us to hear the word of God in Jesus' acts of ministry.

From his being as the Son of God, and from his doing as a fleshly expression of God, we learn two modes of GodSpeech. But Jesus does more than this: he also speaks to us in words, and these words, he asserts, come from God. On one occasion he asks his disciples, "Do you not believe that I am in the Father and the Father is in me? The words that I say to you I do not speak on my own; but the Father who dwells in me does his works" (John 14:10). Jesus asserts that God speaks through his speech.

A review of Jesus' teaching on the mountainside, his parables, and his brief sayings reveal the ways in which God spoke through his speech. The encounter with God through his words, like his being and his doing, is open to a wide spectrum of interpretation. The teaching articulates ideas and principles, but it requires daring acts of imagination to interpret them in particular situations. For example, what does it mean to love the Lord our God with all our heart in the midst of an abusive marriage? What does it mean to love our children when they fall short of our expectations and rebel against our guidance? The rule of love does not shape the expression of love, but Jesus' words provide hints and suggestions.

The Death and Resurrection of Jesus

When Jesus went to Jerusalem for the last time, he drove the sellers and the money changers from the temple. His cleansing of the temple united the opposition and raised their anger to fever pitch. In response to the growing hostility, Jesus asked, "Have you never read in the scriptures: 'The stone that the builders rejected has become the cornerstone; this was the Lord's doing, and it is amazing in our eyes'?" (Matt. 21:42). The events that resulted in Jesus' death occurred in rapid succession. First Judas betrayed him. Next the Jews accused him. And then the Romans crucified him.

On the third day after his crucifixion, Jesus arose from death. Two women who went to the tomb to mourn his death heard these words from a heavenly messenger: "Do not be afraid; I know that you are looking for Jesus who was crucified. He is not here; for he has been raised, as he said" (Matt. 28:5).

Jesus' voluntary act of giving himself to be killed conveys the love of God in an inexpressible manner and surpasses any word that could be spoken to describe God's love. Holy God took on human flesh and willingly suffered death to atone for our sin and rebellion. And the Resurrection shouts the conquest of death. Faith in Christ unites us with him in all times and places, and he sustains us as God's Word to us today. "Because I live, you also will live!" (John 14:19).

In Jesus of Nazareth, God came among us. In Jesus, God took on our nature, shared our pain, and made the ultimate sacrifice for us, thereby giving us hope. The Presence and Word of the Holy One are hidden in Jesus and give his life, teaching, and ministry its parabolic power. Doesn't the designation of Jesus as the parable of God offer a way of seeing the depth of his communication of God to us?

God's speech not only echoes from the past; it is also still heard through the Presence and the Voice that speaks to us today. This Presence and this Voice are most clearly perceived in the church, the body of Christ. We turn next to this speech of the Spirit for further illumination.

QUESTIONS FOR REFLECTION AND DISCUSSION
1. What does it mean to say that "Jesus is the Speech of God"?
2. How is Jesus the parable of God?
3. What are the ways in which GodSpeech occurred through Jesus?
4. What is it about the concept of Jesus as the Speech of God that speaks to you personally?

SUGGESTIONS FOR JOURNALING

Complete the following sentences:

1. I began to experience God's affirmation of my personhood when . . .
2. My deepest struggle with doubt has been . . .
3. In Jesus I discovered that God speaks through . . .
4. One way for me to learn the language of God through the parable of Jesus would be . . .

CHAPTER THREE

GodSpeech through the Spirit

The voice of the LORD is powerful; the voice of the LORD is full of majesty.

Psalm 29:4

The life and ministry of Jesus as the parable of God speak in a manner that is comprehensive, inclusive, and highly concentrated. Examining the metaphorical aspects of this form of GodSpeech provides us with what God speaks to humankind, but it comes in thick, heavy, dense paragraphs that require interpretation.

The church, which is his community, has spent centuries seeking to interpret the Incarnation. God spoke in Jesus a divine/human Word so full of complexity and meaning that we are still trying to grasp its full import more than twenty centuries later. We look at the signs that accompanied Jesus' ministry — healing, feeding, discerning — and seek to appropriate their meaning for our age. We ponder his words and imagine how we might follow them today. Even as we struggle, we believe that Jesus, the Christ, guides us through the maze of questions that take us to the heart of God's message.

This Word spoken in the flesh of Jesus provides the foundation for what God intended in the church and its mission to the world. The Jesus parable is both foundational and paradigmatic for the corporate body, his body on earth, the church. Jesus embodies the speech of God to the world.

The church continues Christ's ministry on earth, and the church must continue listening to Christ to inform its call, direction, and work in the world. Once it becomes clear to us that the church is his body and that he indwells the church through the ages, the necessity of looking to him and listening for him becomes even more urgent. If the church is an organism and not merely an organization, then it draws its life from the source of all life, Christ. Not only is he the source of the community's life, but he is also the Head that directs and inspires its speech.

The book of Acts records a transitional period in the life of the church when the God who first spoke to Abraham, and then spoke in Jesus, began employing the Holy Spirit as the divine speaker of the Word. The account in Acts of the early church reveals how gradually the focus shifted from Jesus to the Holy Spirit as the agent revealing God's presence and will. The Spirit who spoke to and through the early church still speaks to and through the church today. The Spirit mediates God's speech in the time between the ascension of Christ and his coming again at the end of the age. Broadly speaking, Christian history can be divided into "The Age of the Father," "The Age of the Son," and "The Age of the Spirit." And at the end of the ages, the Son through the Spirit will offer the Kingdom to the Father, who will be all and in all.

Pentecost and the Birth of the Church

The Christian feast of Pentecost falls on the day that the Jews celebrate the Feast of Weeks, a time of thanksgiving for the harvest. This commemoration occurs fifty days after the resurrection of Jesus. After his resurrection, Jesus manifested himself to his disciples for forty days, and for ten days the disciples prayed and waited for the coming of the Spirit whom Jesus had promised. On the fiftieth day the Spirit came upon the waiting disciples. The Spirit formed them into a vital, dynamic community and empowered them to hear GodSpeech and proclaim it, to the great awe and amazement of others.

Understanding three precedents to the miracle of Pentecost will help us more fully appreciate what occurred that day. The first incident that illuminates Pentecost is the visit of God's messenger to Mary, the mother of Jesus. He announced to her that she would become pregnant through the ministration of the Spirit and that she would bear in her womb the Son of God. The Annunciation anticipates what happened at Pentecost: the Spirit came upon the disciples of Jesus and formed them into his body on earth. The church, like the womb of the Virgin Mary, bears within itself the Spirit of Christ, making it his corporate earthly body. Through this earthly "form of his existence," to use Karl Barth's phrase, Christ continues his being and doing and speaking in the world. The church is a corporate expression of Jesus Christ that continues his ministry by being what he makes us, doing what he calls us to do, and speaking what he reveals to us.

The second event that contributes to our understanding of the miracle of Pentecost derives from Jesus' final discourse with his disciples. The Apostle John records this final teaching in chapters 14-17 of his gospel. This entire discourse should be interpreted as preparation for the coming of the Spirit. The full exploration of this text is not our purpose, but we can get the seminal idea by closely examining John 14:15-25. If the disciples will obey Jesus' commandments, he will pray to the Father to give them the gift of the Spirit (vv. 15-16). He speaks of the Holy Spirit as "the Spirit of truth." The Spirit will come to them and not to the world (at least not in a way the world will be aware of) because the world "neither sees him nor knows him" (v. 17) and therefore does not receive the Spirit. But the Spirit abides with the disciples in the person of Jesus and will be in them as a living presence after the Ascension. The disciples will discern the Spirit because they have known Christ, and in the Spirit, Christ will remain with them forever.

Jesus promises not to leave them "orphaned." He will come back to them. This pledge refers not only to his second coming in clouds of glory but also to his coming immediately in the Spirit at Pentecost. He says, "On that day you will know that I am in my Father, and you in me, and I in you" (14:20). Thus Pentecost marks the incarnation of the risen Christ in the community of his followers, just as Jesus was the Incarnation of the Word of God in the womb of Mary. And just as Jesus was God's speech to the world, so his followers will be God's speech to the world. As the Father was in the Son, so the Son will be in his followers, both speaking and acting through them.

The third event that illuminates the meaning of Pentecost shines through the ascension of Jesus. I cannot write of the Ascension without visualizing in my mind that place on the hill overlooking the Holy City from which Jesus ascended to heaven (so Christians have believed for centuries). Today a small Islamic mosque sits on the spot, but on numerous occasions I have given its keeper a few shekels so that I and the group of pilgrims I have taken with me could spend a precious half-hour there.

Inside the mosque, my group and I have read again that first chapter of Acts describing Christ's departure. We have listened again to the commission to go into the world as his witnesses, and we have been assured of his presence with us. How could this worshipful moment take place with any degree of integrity if Christ is not present among us, empowering us to fulfill his mission?

To comprehend how Christ remains present among us, we must have a proper understanding of the Ascension. When Jesus was on earth in the flesh, he could only be in one place at one time. The Ascension freed him from this limitation, and when he and the Father poured out the Spirit, he took up residence in the lives of his followers and their community. And the Spirit was poured out not only upon the community but also upon the whole cosmos. Joel, a prophet whom Peter quotes in his Pentecost sermon, promised that the Spirit would be poured out "upon all flesh" (1:17), not merely upon God's people. Thus, through the Holy Spirit, Jesus became a universal presence. And whereas Jesus could only be in one place at one time, the ascended Christ who came again in the fullness of the Holy Spirit could be in all places at all times. So the historical life of Jesus was made universal and continuous in the coming of the Spirit.

Against this background, visualize the account of the miracle of Pentecost:

When the day of Pentecost had come, they were all together in one place. And suddenly from heaven there came a sound like the rush of a violent wind, and it filled the entire house where they were sitting. Divided tongues, as of fire, appeared among them, and a tongue rested on each of them. All of them were filled with the Holy Spirit and began to speak in other languages, as the Spirit gave them ability.

Now there were devout Jews from every nation under heaven living in Jerusalem. And at this sound the crowd gathered and was bewildered, because each one heard them speaking in the native language of each. (Acts 2:1-6)

For ten days these followers of Jesus prepared for the coming of the Spirit. They prayed, anticipated, and committed themselves to God in obedience to Christ. Their expectation was fulfilled in a sudden and dramatic way when the divine presence came, blowing like the wind and burning like fire, and they were filled with holy awe. The Spirit inspired their testimony, and people from seventeen different nations in the Mediterranean world understood the followers' utterances in their own language. In this way the followers began immediately to fulfill Jesus' commission to be his witnesses to the ends of the earth. The first act of the Spirit was to fill Christ's followers with a powerful sense of his presence in and with them; the immediate second act was to fill these faithful with celebrative and testimonial utterances.

This same Spirit would in the future issue calls to ministry — recall the first missionary journey. The Spirit would also provide hope and encouragement to people like Paul — remember his turbulent voyage to Rome — and give personal direction to disciples like Philip, who spoke to the Ethiopian eunuch in the desert.

Pentecost illustrates how the ministry of the Spirit never seems to be directed exclusively to the joy and fulfillment of individuals, but to the calling, equipping, and sending of disciples into ministry to the world. Yet what could be more joyous and fulfilling than to know that you were doing God's will?

Pentecost also demonstrates how the Spirit creates a community.

Through the reception of the Spirit, the disciples were joined not only to Christ but also to one another, linked by a common bond. The Spirit made the community a bearer of the presence of Christ in the world, and Christ continued his work through them. The Spirit bestowed upon each member of the body a gift from Christ, a spiritual capability to express some aspect of Christ's mission and love.

I believe that the early church experienced being Christ's body on earth in a very simple, natural fashion. When they gathered for worship or fellowship after Pentecost, I can imagine their sitting together, praying and discussing the mission. Suddenly John might say to Peter, "I hear the urgency of Christ our Lord in what you said." And Peter might respond to John, "And when you were speaking about the poor in Jerusalem, I heard the compassion of Jesus coming from your heart and your lips." After a few weeks of experiencing Christ in each brother and sister, James might have said, "It's just like having him here with us, because a part of him lives in each one of us." The fullness of Christ existed in no individual believer, but he was fully manifest in the community that bore his name.

What Jesus had begun in his fleshly existence, he continued in the ministry of his followers. Although Pentecost was a singular event, the church in age after age has received fresh outpourings of the Presence — and is experiencing a fresh outpouring of the Spirit today.

The Marks of the Transitional Community

The movement from the parabolic speech in Jesus to the intuitive, inspired speech of the Spirit did not occur instantaneously but emerged gradually as the disciples became more fully aware of the Presence. During the first few years of the church's life, the point of contact shifted from the risen Jesus to the abiding presence of the Spirit. This shift notwithstanding, Christ's followers still regularly invoked the power of his name. And in an effort to carry on his work in the church and the world, they sought to discern the divine word to them. The terms and descriptions of these encounters and actions can enrich our understanding of GodSpeech and its discernment.

Experiencing the Shift from the Risen Christ
to the Abiding Spirit

The Risen Christ   For forty days after his passion, Jesus moved in
and out among his followers, giving them "convincing proofs" that he
was alive and present in the world. During this period he made it clear to
his followers that he intended to establish a spiritual kingdom for all
people, not an earthly kingdom for Israel. In this context, "spiritual"
does not mean "immaterial" but instead suggests a sphere of divine op-
eration that transcends all earthly kingdoms and is entered through the
Spirit. To empower them to fulfill his kingdom mission, Jesus said to his
disciples, "You will receive power when the Holy Spirit has come upon
you; and you will be my witnesses in Jerusalem, in all Judea and Samaria,
and to the ends of the earth" (Acts 1:8). And that was his final word to
them. "When he had said this, as they were watching, he was lifted up,
and a cloud took him out of their sight" (Acts 1:9).

After his ascension into the presence of God, we do not see Jesus on
earth again; we await his second coming in power and great glory. In the
early chapters of Acts, he speaks through visions and by voice a few
times. For example, when Stephen was being stoned, "he gazed into
heaven and saw the glory of God and Jesus standing at the right hand of
God. 'Look,' he said, 'I see the heavens opened and the Son of Man
standing at the right hand of God!'"(Acts 7:55-56). By recalling and describing this event, Luke, the author of Acts, shows us the confidence
that the early church had in Jesus' being at God's right hand but also ob-
servant of and engaged in their life and work on earth. He had departed
physically, but he was still with them spiritually, still aware of the plight
of his followers. Speaking to them through Stephen's vision gave them
this assurance.

This awareness of the risen Christ being actively engaged in the life
of the church received increased assurance from the experience of Saul
of Tarsus. His life's course was changed when the risen Christ spoke to
him on the road to Damascus. As he journeyed, a light from heaven suddenly flashed around him, blinding him, and he fell to the ground. Then
a voice spoke to him:

"Saul, Saul, why do you persecute me?"

He asked, "Who are you, Lord?"

The reply came, "I am Jesus, whom you are persecuting. But get up and enter the city, and you will be told what you are to do." (Acts 9:5-6)

Saul's encounter with Jesus complements Stephen's vision — but Christ not only appeared to Saul but also spoke to him and directed his path. The followers of Christ in Damascus received new strength and assurance from the testimony of Saul. Saul now believed in Jesus because the Voice from heaven had confronted and changed him. If the risen Jesus spoke to Saul, the followers reasoned, surely he was their ally, and he would be speaking to others who opposed the young movement.

The risen Jesus also intervened in the life of a disciple in Damascus. Ananias was most likely an elder in the church at Damascus, and a few days after Saul's experience on the road, the Lord spoke to him in a vision:

"Ananias."

He answered, "Here I am, Lord."

The Lord said to him, "Get up and go to the street called Straight, and at the house of Judas look for a man of Tarsus named Saul. At this moment he is praying, and he has seen in a vision a man named Ananias come in and lay his hands on him so that he might regain his sight."

But Ananias answered, "Lord, I have heard from many about this man, how much evil he has done to your saints in Jerusalem; and here he has authority from the chief priests to bind all who invoke your name."

But the Lord said to him, "Go, for he is an instrument whom I have chosen to bring my name before Gentiles and kings and before the people of Israel; I myself will show him how much he must suffer for the sake of my name."

So Ananias went and entered the house. He laid his hands on

Saul and said, "Brother Saul, the Lord Jesus, who appeared to you on your way here, has sent me so that you may regain your sight and be filled with the Holy Spirit." (Acts 9:10-17)

This report further reveals how the risen Christ was at work in his church. On the road to Damascus, he spoke directly to Saul. In Damascus he spoke to Ananias in a vision, and he commissioned Saul through the words of this layman. Ananias not only spoke with Saul about Christ's intention for him; he also baptized the great apostle. Although Ananias was at first reluctant to do God's bidding, in the end he accepted the commission and communicated Christ's intention to Saul. When Saul later said that Jesus spoke with him about his mission to the Gentiles, he was referring to the words spoken by Ananias, through which Christ himself spoke.

So it appears that the risen Christ increasingly spoke both to his followers and to outsiders through the lips of those who knew and followed him. Still, Saul — also known as Paul — seems to have retained the sense that Jesus was speaking directly to him. Later on he reported, "After I had returned to Jerusalem and while I was praying in the temple, I fell into a trance and saw Jesus saying to me, 'Hurry and get out of Jerusalem quickly, because they will not accept your testimony about me'" (Acts 22:17-18).

Peter also experienced the Voice speaking directly to him. He was residing at Simon the tanner's house, and about noon one day he went up to the rooftop to pray. While on the rooftop, "he became hungry and wanted something to eat; and while it was being prepared, he fell into a trance" (Acts 10:10). He saw a sheet descending from heaven filled with ritually unclean animals. In the midst of this trance he heard a voice speak to him:

"Get up, Peter; kill and eat."

But Peter said, "By no means, Lord; for I have never eaten anything that is profane or unclean."

The voice said to him again, a second time, "What God has made clean, you must not call profane."

This happened three times, and the thing was suddenly taken up to heaven.

Now while Peter was greatly puzzled about what to make of the vision that he had seen, suddenly the men sent by Cornelius appeared. They were asking for Simon's house and were standing by the gate. (Acts 10:13-17)

Peter's experience of GodSpeech involved both voice and vision. When the vision of unclean animals appeared before him, the Voice spoke. Peter believed the word came from the voice of the risen Christ, and that he was being instructed to eat food that he, as a Jew, had been forbidden to eat all his life. Overcoming his abhorrence of these unclean creatures and his lifetime of abstinence required a strongly convincing word from Christ.

Peter's wonderment about the vision and the Voice received almost immediate clarification. At the gate of Simon's house stood three men sent by Cornelius, the Roman centurion who was a believer. They had come to invite him to meet the centurion. The appearance of the three messengers correlated with the vision and the Voice that Peter had experienced. They had removed the obstacle of "uncleanness" and prepared him to go to a Gentile's house.

We learn two important characteristics of GodSpeech — we might call these rules of grammar — from the incidents I have described. First, God speaks to us through inward visions like Peter's trance, which may or may not be accompanied by explanatory words. And second, an external invitation to ministry correlates with this internal vision. These two characteristics often mark a call to a particular ministry. The call begins with an internal image and a voice speaking to us. For example, we may find the needs of abused children occupying our thoughts, and the Voice that we hear calls us to begin the work of helping them. At the time that we feel the call, a door opens for us so that we can begin our service. Here two aspects of GodSpeech come together — call and opportunity, both the speech of God. The voice of Christ in our hearts parallels the opportunity to obey.

Luke, the first compiler of the history of the early church, gives other instances when the risen Lord spoke to Paul. In Corinth, for example, an official and his family became believers in Christ, and their conversion stirred up animosity among the Jews. When Paul became fearful for his life, the risen Christ said to him, "Do not be afraid, but speak and do not be silent; for I am with you, and no one will lay a hand on you to harm you, for there are many in this city who are my people" (Acts 18:9-10). On another reported occasion, when Paul was in Jerusalem, Christ warned him to leave the city.

What do these reports of the risen Christ speaking to his followers teach us about his engagement with the church today?

The Spirit of the Lord The story of the Pentecostal church gives us insight into the working of the Spirit as well as the transition from the risen Jesus to the Spirit as the primary divine agent. Take, for instance, the experience of Philip, one of Jesus' disciples. In the post-Pentecost days, Philip proclaimed Christ to the Samaritans. When he had finished his work in this community, an angel of the Lord said to him, "Get up and go toward the south to the road that goes down from Jerusalem to Gaza" (8:26). There he encountered an Ethiopian eunuch who was the treasurer of Candace, queen of the Ethiopians. This convert to the faith was returning from worshipping in Jerusalem.

The Spirit said to Philip, "Go over to this chariot and join it" (8:29). Philip did as he was instructed. After a conversation with the eunuch about the text from Isaiah that he was reading, Philip baptized him. Then Philip was "spirited away": "When they came up out of the water, the Spirit of the Lord snatched Philip away; the eunuch saw him no more, and went on his way rejoicing" (8:39).

Two important insights come to us from this account. First, Philip's experience demonstrates that the risen Lord is still directing the work of the church. Second, the "language" is shifting from Jesus leading the believers to the Spirit's providing guidance. True, it is the Spirit of the Lord, but no vision of the risen Lord occurs here — just very clear directives.

The Angel of the Lord References to "the angel of the Lord" in the book of Acts raise interesting questions. Who is the angel of the Lord?

We know that "angel" means "messenger." God sent an angel to announce the birth of Christ, to reassure Joseph about Mary, and to comfort Christ in his sufferings. In the early church, the angel of the Lord directed Peter and John to go to the temple to preach, sent Philip toward Gaza, and appeared to Cornelius the centurion. In the book of Acts the angel of the Lord delivers God's messages to God's people. Usually the message is closely connected with an aspect of the church's mission.

After John and Peter had been imprisoned by the Sadducees for preaching and performing miracles, they were put before the council and interrogated. But Peter, "filled with the Holy Spirit," answered the council members so resoundingly that he and John were let go. But because they continued to preach and perform acts of healing, they were arrested and imprisoned again. During the night, however, the angel of the Lord opened the prison doors and instructed them, "Go, stand in the temple and tell the people the whole message about this life" (5:20). When the prison officials reported to the Sadducees that the two were back in the temple preaching, it created no small stir.

Cornelius, the Gentile believer who eventually met Peter, had a vision that shook him, as Luke reports:

> One afternoon at about three o'clock he had a vision in which he clearly saw an angel of God coming in and saying to him, "Cornelius."
>
> He stared at him in terror and said, "What is it, Lord?"
>
> He answered, "Your prayers and your alms have ascended as a memorial before God. Now send men to Joppa for a certain Simon who is called Peter." (10:3-5)

At this time Cornelius did not know Christ, but he knew God. So when he reported his vision, he used the term "the angel of God." It appears from this and other reports that "the angel of the Lord," "the angel of God," and "the Spirit of the Lord" are interchangeable in the Acts narrative. These various expressions indicate that the young church was searching for a vocabulary to describe Christ's continuing disclosures after the Ascension. Recognizing this gradual shift from Jesus to the

Spirit is important to our understanding of the multifaceted language of God.

Invoking the Name of Jesus Christ   In the book of Acts, invoking the name of Jesus suggests yet another mode of God's speech. To speak in the name of Jesus meant to speak with the authority of Jesus or to speak in Jesus' stead. So when Peter and John encountered the lame beggar at the gate of the temple, they had no money to give him, but they did have the power of Christ. Peter said to the man, "I have no silver or gold, but what I have I give you; in the name of Jesus Christ of Nazareth, stand up and walk" (3:6). After issuing this command, Peter "took him by the right hand and raised him up; and immediately his feet and ankles were made strong" (3:7).

As an apostle of Christ, Peter spoke the word of Christ to the lame man. It was as though Christ himself commanded the man to stand up and walk. When Peter acted in Christ's name, his speech was GodSpeech and manifested the power of Christ.

The same kind of healing occurred through Jesus' name when Peter came to Lydda, where he met a man who had been paralyzed for years. "Peter said to him, 'Aeneas, Jesus Christ heals you; get up and make your bed!' And immediately he got up" (Acts 9:34).

Paul also spoke in Jesus' name when he went to Philippi and preached Christ. In that city a slave girl who "had a spirit of divination" had made her owners rich by telling fortunes. She began following Paul, who was there with Silas, and shouting at the top of her lungs, "These men are slaves of the Most High God, who proclaim to you a way of salvation" (16:17). She followed them for many days. Finally, Paul, who was very irritated, turned and said to the perverse spirit in her, "I order you in the name of Jesus Christ to come out of her" (16:18). And that very hour the woman was liberated.

GodSpeech comes through people who have been filled with the Spirit of Christ and are empowered by him to speak in his name. In his name they proclaim the message of salvation, they speak words of healing, and they cast out evil spirits. Although we often do not know when Christ is using our speech, we still dare to speak in his name.

Practicing Corporate Discernment   In the book of Acts, Luke describes an abortive attempt at discernment as well as numerous accurate discernments, and also gives us one guiding principle from outside the faith. Each instance instructs us in the way of GodSpeech.

First, recall the unsuccessful discernment of the apostles when they sought a successor to Judas. Jesus had originally chosen twelve men, and one of them had fallen and then taken his own life. The apostles sought to replace Judas with a twelfth witness to the life, ministry, death, and resurrection of Jesus. After enumerating the requirements for an apostle, they selected two from among the followers: Justus and Matthias.

> Then they prayed and said, "Lord, you know everyone's heart. Show us which one of these two you have chosen to take the place in this ministry and apostleship from which Judas turned aside to go to his own place." And they cast lots for them, and the lot fell on Matthias; and he was added to the eleven apostles. (Acts 1:24-26)

Doubtless this was not an accurate discernment. For one thing, we never hear of Matthias again. He sinks into oblivion in the New Testament record. And for another, Paul testified that Christ made him an apostle — and there is no reason to doubt this assertion. He was known to the others, he ministered in the early church — and he was chosen by Christ himself (Rom. 1:1-6).

From this failed effort at discernment we should learn that we do not always discern correctly. We can do everything in our power to listen to God and to see his hand, and still be mistaken. We are human and thus not perfect. Good intentions do not equal good judgment. And sometimes God performs his will even when we do not recognize it at the time — as when God made Paul an apostle.

An accurate discernment of the Spirit seems to have occurred at Antioch, a thriving city in Syria. Key representatives of the church had gathered there. While they were worshipping and fasting, the Holy Spirit said to them, "Set apart for me Barnabas and Saul for the work to which I have called them" (13:2). The small group of five heard the call of the Spirit to extend the mission. After further fasting and praying, they "laid hands on" the two men the Spirit had named and sent them forth to proclaim the gospel. Note that in this instance discernment took place in a context of worship, prayer, and fasting. Not every act of discernment occurs in this context, but the first missionary expedition did arise out of such a situation.

Another instance of discernment occurred after Peter preached the gospel to Cornelius and his household in Caesarea. When Peter returned to Jerusalem, the leaders of the young church questioned him: "Why did you go to uncircumcised men and eat with them?" (Acts 11:3). In this instance discernment began with a perceived irregularity: a Jew like Peter was not supposed to associate with Gentiles. Peter responded by telling his questioners exactly what had happened. After his vision in Joppa, Cornelius's men came knocking at the gate. "The Spirit told me to go with them," he explained, "and not to make a distinction between them and us" (11:12). So he went to Caesarea with the men, taking six companions with him. When they arrived at Cornelius's house, he discovered that Cornelius had been visited by an angel with a very specific message: "Send to Joppa and bring Simon, who is called Peter; he will give you a message by which your entire household will be saved" (11:13-14). So Peter preached to them, and, he recalled, "the Holy Spirit fell upon them just as it had upon us at the beginning [Pentecost]" (11:15). How could he reject God's will in these circumstances? "If then God gave them the same gift that he gave us when we believed in the Lord Jesus Christ, who was I that I could hinder God?" (11:17). When his questioners heard Peter's explanation, "they were silenced. And they praised God, saying, 'Then God has given even to the Gentiles the repentance that leads to life'" (11:18).

This instance of corporate spiritual discernment provides a helpful model for today. When an issue arises, the church should gather the pertinent data, examine its authority for the action in question, hear the evidence of God's involvement in the situation, consult with each other, and seek to make decisions that accomplish the mission of Christ.

One other instance in Acts is worthy of note: the advice of Gamaliel. When Peter and John were before the council a second time, after they had been found preaching in the temple again, the council sought to silence them. The exchanges between the council and the apostles grew heated, and Gamaliel, a Pharisee who was one of the council members, ordered that the men be removed from the hearing for a short time.

After they left, Gamaliel, a man highly respected by all, related two instances when zealots had attracted followers. In both cases the leaders had perished, and their followers had dispersed. Then came his discernment: "So in the present case, I tell you, keep away from these men and let them alone; because if this plan or this undertaking is of human origin, it will fail; but if it is of God, you will not be able to overthrow them — in that case you may even be found fighting against God!" (5:38-39).

I wonder if it would be wise for the church today to wait and see the results of changes and innovations before pronouncing judgment. Perhaps we need the wisdom of Gamaliel!

What This Means for Us

This review of life in the early church suggests that the risen Christ has taken up residence in the community of the faithful, his body on earth. Through the Holy Spirit, Christ continues to speak to his church, empower it, and guide it in his mission to the world. We are the contemporary expression of that Spirit-baptized church of the book of Acts, and we have the same mission of bearing witness to Christ and doing his work in the world. As surely as Christ continued to guide the early church, he will guide us in his mission now — and how we respond to him is crucial for the life of the church today.

The most important task of the twenty-first-century church is to learn to listen for Christ. The mission of the church receives its primary impetus from the call of God, not the need of the world. To discern the call of God, we must learn the language of God, and this means dealing directly with the awesome presence of the Holy One in our midst.

QUESTIONS FOR REFLECTION AND DISCUSSION

1. What three events give clarity and perspective to the Pentecost event?
2. How would you describe the transition from the risen Jesus to the abiding Spirit in the book of Acts?
3. What are characteristic ways that the Spirit speaks?
4. How can we encourage the work of the Spirit in our corporate ministry in the church?

SUGGESTIONS FOR JOURNALING

1. Find a quiet place to sit and relax. Put yourself in a receptive frame of mind and read three times the story of the Spirit's coming at Pentecost (Acts 2:1-4). Sit quietly with your thoughts, then record them.
2. Write an imaginative, first-person account of Pentecost, describing the experience of the Spirit's coming as if you had been sitting in the group and awaiting the Spirit.
3. Write a letter to God in which you request divine help in opening your life fully to the divine presence.

The Historical Development

GodSpeech: From Polycarp
to Julian of Norwich

The voice of the LORD breaks the cedars; the LORD breaks the cedars of Lebanon. He makes Lebanon skip like a calf, and Sirion like a young wild ox.

Psalm 29:5-6

The God who spoke continues to speak! What I have written about the speech of God up to this point falls within the bounds of the tradition's theological emphases and congregational expectations: God spoke to Abraham, God spoke in Christ, and God continues to speak through the Spirit. I have also examined the characteristics of the Spirit's speaking in the book of Acts. The church needs to go beyond this normative emphasis on GodSpeech, however, and attend the continuing speech of God. God did not cease speaking at the close of the scriptural canon. An examination of the lives of leading religious figures from the ancient church to the present sustains this claim. Engagement with the living Christ did not cease with the death of the last apostle. In all the centuries that follow, we find person after person giving clear and passionate witness to Christ's word to them through the Spirit. In addition to those whom we can name, there was surely a multitude of ordinary persons who heard his voice and followed his way, persons whose names are not recorded in the annals of spiritual history.

I have personally benefited from an examination of the experiences of those preachers, teachers, mystics, and ordinary people who through the ages heard God speak to them, and I pass on to you a summary of my findings.

Polycarp
c. 80-155

The Apostolic Fathers, as they are called, were a group of early Christian writers who succeeded the apostles. One of these successors was Polycarp, venerable bishop of the church in Smyrna. Perhaps his martyrdom for Christ etched his name permanently in the mind of the second-century church. In the post-apostolic church, martyrdom represented the highest form of spirituality and one kind of union with the risen Christ.

Ignatius and Origen, for example, looked upon martyrdom both as a sacrament and as a kind of second coming of Jesus. They thought of martyrdom as a sacrament because this sacrificial act mediated the presence of Christ in the same way that the bread and wine did. And they claimed it as a form of the second coming of Jesus because he always came to those who gave their lives for him. Christ's presence to the saints when they were being martyred for his sake speaks to our concern. His presence assured them of the conquest of death and their immediate resurrection.

Perhaps nothing in the first few centuries of the church's life held greater significance for believers and faithful Christians than the strange yet reassuring events that surrounded the witness of martyrs. For them it was the most intimate experience of Christ that anyone on earth could have. According to Louis Boyer, "Martyrdom appeared as the greatest charismatic experience in the ancient church."[1] After the report of Stephen's martyrdom in the book of Acts, we next find in the detailed account of the martyrdom of Polycarp a very powerful example of one who gave his life for Christ.

1. Boyer, *The Spirituality of the New Testament* (New York: Seabury, 1982), p. 204.

Polycarp was one of the early combatants against Christian heresy, and the Roman authorities eventually decided to arrest him, claiming that he was a member of a dangerous cult. When Polycarp learned that the authorities were coming for him, he intended to do nothing to hinder them. But his followers persuaded him to take refuge in a farmhouse, hoping that he wouldn't be arrested. While in seclusion, Polycarp prayed night and day for all people and especially for the church throughout the world.

One day while he was worshipping, Polycarp fell into a trance and had a vision in which his pillow was on fire. After the vision he told his friends, "It must be that I shall be burned alive." Again, at the insistence of his followers, he departed to another place of seclusion.

When the authorities searched his first place of refuge, they didn't find him. But Herod, the head of the authorities, tortured two slave boys until they told him where to find Polycarp. Herod was intent on arresting Polycarp and presenting him to the authorities.

Late in the night the police converged on the farm where Polycarp was in hiding. The old man was asleep. Although his companions had again admonished him to move on, he had refused. He had said simply, "The will of God be done."

Upon hearing that the authorities had come, Polycarp went downstairs and greeted them. Then he instructed that a table be set for them, and he encouraged them to eat their fill. As they were sitting down to their meal, he asked that he be given an hour to pray, a request that was granted. This remarkable hospitality made his captors feel guilty, and they repented that they had come to arrest the saintly old man.

When he had prayed and they had eaten, they seated Polycarp on a donkey and brought him into the city. At the city's edge, Herod and his father, Nicetes, took him into their carriage and made a final plea: "What harm is there in saying, 'Caesar is Lord'?"

No answer. They persisted.

Finally Polycarp answered, "I am not going to do what you counsel me."

Herod rebuked Polycarp, threatened him, and demanded that he get out of the carriage. He bruised his flesh as he stepped down. Then he was taken to the Roman stadium, where the noise was so great that a man couldn't even hear his own voice. But as the bishop entered the stadium, a louder voice spoke from heaven: "Polycarp, play the man." None saw who spoke, but those who accompanied Polycarp heard the voice.

The proconsul asked, "Are you the man?"

Polycarp answered simply, "Yes."

Whereupon the proconsul said, "Repent, confess Caesar, and say, 'Away with the atheists'!"

Instead of denouncing the Christians, Polycarp gazed at the masses gathered to observe his martyrdom, and as he motioned toward them, he said, "Away with the atheists!"

Again, the magistrate urged, "Swear the oath to Caesar and revile Christ."

In response, Polycarp gave a witness that has echoed down through the ages: "Four score and six years I have been his servant, and he has done me no wrong. How can I blaspheme my king who saved me?"

The magistrate, not desiring Polycarp's death, kept pleading with him to say the oath.

Polycarp again responded, "You act as if you are ignorant of who I am. Hear me clearly: I am a Christian."

"If you will not listen to me, appeal to the crowd," the magistrate pleaded.

"I am willing to speak with you, for we have been taught to honor leaders as appointed by God, but as for these" — and he swept his arm around the stadium — "I do not hold them worthy that I should defend myself before them."

"I have wild beasts here, and I can call for them."

"Call for them."

"I will cause you to be consumed by fire!"

"You light the fire that burns for a moment and do not consider the fire of the judgment and eternal punishment. Why do you delay? Do what you will!"[2]

---

2. "The Martyrdom of Polycarp," in *The Apostolic Fathers,* edited and translated by J. B. Lightfoot (Grand Rapids: Baker Book House, 1962), pp. 112-13.

At this challenge, the magistrate commanded that wood be brought and piled around Polycarp. When the executioners were about to nail him to the stake, he asked them not to drive the nails into his flesh. "He who will sustain me through the fire will help me to remain in the pile unmoved." They tied him to the stake instead.

The bishop prayed, and when he had finished, the executioners lit the fire. A mighty flame burst forth. It looked like a vault, like the sail of a ship filled with wind, and it formed a wall around the body of the martyr. He was there in the midst of the flames, not like flesh burning but like a loaf baking in the oven.

After a while, the men who lit the fire saw that Polycarp was not consumed, so they stabbed him with a dagger, and his blood quenched the fire. At this moment, his disciple Irenaeus, who happened to be in the city, heard a voice like a trumpet saying, "Polycarp is martyred."

Perhaps comparing the martyrdom of Polycarp to the death of Christ only marginally relates to my assertion that God still speaks, but there is, nevertheless, a similarity between the two. Like Christ, Polycarp was interrogated at length before being led to his death. He was repeatedly urged to deny Christ, just as Christ was challenged again and again to recant his claim to be the Son of God. As the thunder sounded when Christ hung on the cross, so the Voice spoke to Polycarp when he entered the stadium. And the vision of Polycarp in the flames has been described in Eucharistic images — like bread baking in an oven. These similarities make it easy for us to see Polycarp as a kind of Christ figure.

No doubt the author and the editors have stylized this recounting of Polycarp's martyrdom, and copyists through the ages have given it many characteristics of hagiography and legend. But there is a consistent witness at the core of this recounting. There is no way to prove the details of this story, but I do believe that God spoke to Polycarp with an assurance that resulted in his inspiring courage. Christ spoke to him, and that word sustained him so that he could face death fearlessly.

Anthony of the Desert
c. 250-355

The story of Anthony sounds strange to modern ears. Here is a man who sold all his possessions, giving the proceeds to the poor, and spent twenty years alone in the desert of Egypt along the Nile River. He is a strange person, but he may have made a major contribution to the sagging faith of many Christians and the preservation of a vital Christianity in the third century.

What we know about Anthony comes from Athanasius, who wrote his biography with an eye toward preparing individuals for the monastic life. In some ways Anthony's choices seem even more radical than those of Bishop Polycarp. Being willing to die for Christ at the stake is something we can understand; choosing to sequester oneself in the desert and in the process suffering death to self and to the world is so radical that it is difficult for us to grasp. Yet these two men represent forms of spirituality that have greatly nourished and transformed the Christian church. Polycarp's faithfulness inspired many of God's people to face persecution, suffering, and death for their faith. And Anthony's journey into the desert marked a trail that thousands followed in pursuit of a life with God. Both represent lives sacrificed to God.

Both of these leaders also listened for and heeded GodSpeech. So both Polycarp and Anthony exemplify the continuation of GodSpeech beyond the apostolic era. Contemplating the specifics of Anthony's life and devotion will show how closely he listened to the Voice.

Anthony was the son of a wealthy family. His parents were Christians who took young Anthony to worship regularly, and from an early age he yearned after God. When he was just twenty years old, both his parents died, and he inherited all their wealth and possessions; his sister also became his responsibility. These circumstances meant that he would have to make hard decisions about his wealth, his sister, and the direction his life would take.

An answer seemed to come to him one Sunday morning when he went to church and heard the reading of the gospel: "If you would be perfect, go, sell what you possess and give to the poor, and you will have treasure in heaven." As Anthony heard these words, originally spoken to the rich young ruler, it was as if the Lord was personally addressing him. He was deeply moved by Christ's invitation, and although confusion filled his mind, he pondered whether the Lord was indeed calling him to forsake all and follow him.

The next day, still engaged in this gut-wrenching struggle, he entered the church to pray and again heard the Lord speak: "Do not be anxious about tomorrow." Convinced that he was hearing God's voice, he went from the church and did as the Voice instructed: he gave all that he had to the poor (with the exception of what he gave to the women who agreed to care for his sister).

After stripping himself of all possessions, he joined a hermit who lived at the edge of the village. In Anthony's day it was rather common for God-seekers to settle outside the community in order to spend their time in prayer without interruption. These hermits often supported themselves by cultivating small gardens for food and weaving reed mats for a little money.

Not only did Anthony attach himself to the hermit near his village; he also traveled about, seeking other men of God from whom he could learn God's ways. His explorations exposed him to saints rich in humility, faith, and spiritual power. In the faces of those whom he met, Anthony saw an image of the kind of person he longed to be. And in his conversations with them, he listened for the confirmation of his call. (The virtues he found in them he would one day exemplify in his own life.)

Finally, being persuaded of his call, he went beyond his contemporaries in seeking seclusion: he left the village and journeyed into the desert. The desert represented a time and place of temptation, testing, and purification, as it did for his Lord, who also entered the desert to clarify his vocation. There he sequestered himself in an old, dilapidated fort. He made this his home, both his place of struggle and the temple where he prayed to God. Thus, as a place of both battle and refuge, the old fort symbolized Anthony's quest.

In the desert he got quiet enough for all of his dark side to surface, and he called these dark revelations "demons." Here he fought the enemy to the death, seeking the release of Satan's grip on his life. Indeed, the struggles that Anthony had with himself and with the devil make up many of the accounts of his experiences in the desert.

In one of his struggles with the devil's minions during the night, he heard loud, crashing noises, felt pain in his body, and was gripped by fear. Yet he responded to the creatures tormenting him, "If you are so powerful, why did two of you come?" He pleaded for the power of the Lord. Suddenly he saw a bright light with its beam descending toward him. Aware that his fear had ceased and that his breathing had slowed, Anthony entreated the vision: "Where were you? Why didn't you appear in the beginning, so that you could stop my distresses?"

And a voice came to him: "I was here, Anthony, but I waited and watched your struggle. And now, since you persevered and were not defeated, I will be your helper forever, and I will make you known everywhere." The Voice that spoke to Anthony in the village church spoke to him again in the desert.[3]

On another occasion Anthony had an encounter with Satan himself. He heard a knock at the door. When he opened it, he saw someone massive and tall. "Who are you?" he asked.

"I am Satan."

"What are you doing here?"

Satan responded with a question. "Why do all the monks and the other Christians censure me without cause? Why do they curse me every hour?"

Anthony also responded with a question. "Why do you torment them?"

Satan answered, "The desert is filled with monks. Let them watch after themselves and quit censuring me."

Then Anthony said to him, "Even though you are a liar and never tell the truth, this time you have not lied. Christ has indeed reduced you to weakness, and after throwing you down has left you defenseless."[4]

---

3. Athanasius, *The Life of Anthony*, edited by Robert C. Gregg (New York: Paulist Press, 1980), p. 39.

4. Athanasius, *The Life of Anthony*, p. 62.

This encounter with Satan shows that the world of the Spirit was as real and as near to Anthony as the air he breathed.

Although Anthony was not the first Christian hermit, he was among the most influential. During the years he spent in the desert, a small colony of would-be disciples took up residence near him. They beseeched him to be their spiritual leader.

After spending nearly twenty years sequestered in his fort, Anthony yielded to these entreaties. Those who saw him beheld a man who was strong and centered. He had not grown weak from fasting or sad from praying. He was not "constricted by grief nor relaxed by pleasure, nor affected by either laughter or dejection."[5]

Soon both church leaders and rulers sought his wisdom. Athanasius tells how Constantine Augustus wrote to Anthony, begging for his guidance. When his disciples were amazed, Anthony simply said, "Do not consider it marvelous. Instead, [consider it marvelous] that God wrote the law for mankind, and has spoken to us through his own Son."[6] At the urging of his disciples, he wrote to the ruler and his son that they should "recognize Christ alone as the true and eternal ruler, . . . be men of human concern, and give attention to justice and to the poor."[7]

In the desert both men and women searched for themselves and for God. Over time, the desert gave birth to the monastic movement, and Anthony became known as the father of Christian monachism. The monastic way has deeply nurtured the hearts and lives of seekers and provided a wealth of devotional material for contemplation.

In Anthony we meet another of those key individuals in the long history of God's speaking to humans. His awakening came through a scriptural text that became the Voice of Christ speaking to him. This voice spoke to him through Scripture again to confirm his sense of calling. He had the courage to follow the Voice into the desert and seek out God and examine the depths of his soul. In so doing he had conversa-

---

5. Athanasius, *The Life of Anthony*, p. 42.
6. Athanasius, *The Life of Anthony*, p. 89.
7. Athanasius, *The Life of Anthony*, p. 90.

tions with the personification of evil as frequently as he had intercourse with God. But always and in every place, God spoke the final word to him and strengthened him in his vocation.

Augustine and Others

From a logical and chronological standpoint, the next person to draw on as an illustration of one to whom God spoke would be Augustine. But since his story as told in *The Confessions* provides a full and penetrating description of the diverse ways in which God speaks to us, I have elected to introduce his experience later.

Leaping from the fourth century to the twelfth makes me somewhat uneasy because I am omitting so many noteworthy individuals in the process — Saint Gregory, Saint John Climacus, Saint Romuald, Saint Peter Damian, and Saint Benedict of Nursia. But a brief survey of GodSpeech prevents me from including all of the people who have been convinced — and convincing — hearers of God.

Francis of Assisi
c. 1182-1226

Perhaps no servant of God has been more completely shaped by a word from God than Francis of Assisi. Like Samuel of old, he heard the Voice and offered himself to God without hesitation. The Voice that spoke to him transformed him, redirecting and reshaping his life.

He was born in 1182, the son of an Italian man, Pietro Bernardone, and his French wife, Lady Pica. Francis's father was a merchant who lived in Assisi but traveled widely, trading in fabrics. Pietro had become wealthy, and young Francis benefited from his father's business success and station in life. He wore fine clothes and spent money lavishly.

At about the age of twenty, inspired by the vision of knighthood, he joined other young men to fight against a neighboring city, Perugia. During the battle he was captured and imprisoned. While he was incarcerated, he contracted tuberculosis, and upon his release he returned to Assisi, where he spent a full year recovering. During that time he walked the hills surrounding the city, grieving his emptiness and lack of joy as his hopes of glory faded.

When his health returned, however, he again attempted to fulfill his vision of knighthood — this time at Spoleto. In a dream he saw the large walls of a castle covered with shields. A voice indicated that the shields belonged to Francis and his followers. Still eager to succeed as a knight, Francis took the message to mean that his dream of knighthood would come true. But the Voice spoke again.

"Francis, is it better to serve the Lord or the servant?"

"O, sir, the Lord, of course."

"Then why are you trying to turn your Lord into a servant?"

Recognizing the Voice, Francis asked, "Lord, what do you want me to do?"

"Return to Assisi. There it will be shown to you the meaning of this vision and what you are to do."[8]

But it took Francis some time to discern what the Voice actually meant. One day, while praying before a crucifix in the decrepit San Damiano chapel, he heard Christ speak to him. It seemed to him that the lips of the crucifix said, "Francis, go and repair my house, which, as you can see, is falling into ruin." Immediately Francis went to Assisi, took a bale of cloth from his father's store, and traveled by horse to a nearby town. He sold both the cloth and the horse and brought the money to the priest at San Damiano, so that the church could be restored. The priest refused to take the money, suspecting that Francis had gotten it by questionable means.

His father, outraged by Francis's behavior, sought to deny him his inheritance. Francis was unperturbed by this turn of events; in fact, he welcomed it. Before an audience that included the bishop, he stripped off the clothes he was wearing and returned them to his father, announcing that henceforth he had only a father in heaven.

For a while afterward, Francis wandered here and there, trying to

8. Murray Bodo, *The Way of St. Francis* (New York: Image Books, 1984), p. 4.

be God's emissary. Eventually, remembering the words that the Voice had spoken to him, he returned to Assisi, begging for stones to repair the old chapel. He did not yet understand what the Voice meant when it said, "Repair my church."[9]

Another episode a year later clarified his vision. He went to Mass and heard a clear word from God. In the Scripture reading for the day he heard these verses from Matthew:

> Do not possess gold, nor silver, nor money in your purses; nor script for your journey, nor two coats, nor shoes nor a staff; for the workman is worthy of his food. And into whatsoever city or town you shall enter, inquire who in it is worthy and there abide till you go thence. (Matt. 10:9-10)[10]

Francis felt that God was speaking directly to him. He immediately divested himself of his few remaining possessions and dressed himself in only a coarse woolen tunic. He then traveled throughout the countryside, exhorting others to love, peace, and penance.

Gradually he developed a significant following, and he drew up a rule of life for them that was approved by the pope (a rule that still guides the life of the Franciscan order today).

After more than a decade of living and working for Christ, Francis went to La Verna to fast in preparation for one of the big feasts of the church. There he prayed earnestly, "O Lord, I beg you for two graces before I die — to experience personally and in all possible fullness the pains of your bitter Passion, and to feel for You the same love that moved You to sacrifice Yourself for us." After Francis offered this prayer, the marks of Christ appeared in his body — in his hands, his feet, and his side. For fifty days thereafter he lived in a spiritual darkness so dense that he prayed, "My God, why have you forsaken me?"

As he struggled with his aloneness, the pain of his wounds, and his weakening eyesight, the Voice finally spoke to him again.

9. Bodo, *The Way of St. Francis,* p. 5.
10. Bodo, *The Way of St. Francis,* p. 7.

"Francis, if in exchange for all these evils, you were to receive a treasure so great that the whole earth, changed into gold, would be nothing beside it, would you not have reason to be satisfied?"

"Certainly, Lord."

"Then be happy, for I guarantee you that one day you shall indeed enjoy the Kingdom of Heaven, and this is as certain as if you possessed it already."[11]

In Francis we encounter a saint different from Polycarp and Anthony. Although both these devout souls heard the Lord speak to them in definitive ways, neither gives us the impression that his life was an ongoing conversation with the Lord — as Francis's life seemed to be. The unassuming man from Assisi has become an icon, a revered representative of the power of GodSpeech for millions of believers. His influence has spanned the centuries, and the order that he founded exists as a reminder that we should always listen for God, because he speaks to ordinary people.

Thomas Aquinas
1225-1274

One of the great doctors of the church, like Albert the Great, Saint Augustine, and Saint Paul, Thomas Aquinas had a profound encounter with God — though it was quite different from the others described here. Thomas was first and foremost a theologian. He took the thought of Aristotle as a framework for his *Summa Theologica,* the most comprehensive theological statement written up to that point in Christian history. In his work he interpreted not only Aristotle but also Neo-Platonism and the thought of several Arabian philosophers. It is also reported that he read daily from the work of John Cassian, the man who introduced monasticism to the West.

Thomas's writing reflected his personal experience of God. It has been reported that he dictated most of the *Summa Theologica* in a state of ecstasy.

---

11. Bodo, *The Way of Saint Francis,* pp. 9-10.

Toward the end of his lifetime, Thomas was granted a vision of the Lord's glory. Afterwards he said, "Compared with what I have seen, everything that I have written seems to me no more than straw."[12]

For the rest of his days, Thomas did not write another word of theology. The beatific vision of God he received — which clearly defied description — may have been as powerful as the visions of the martyred saints.

In Thomas we meet a man who was highly intelligent and rational but also listened for God in a personal and subjective way. In him we see that reason and spiritual experience are not mutually exclusive. Indeed, he argued for the co-existence of faith and reason, insisting that reason could operate within faith and yet remain consistent with its own laws.

Increasingly it should be dawning on us that God's speech cannot be limited to biblical times; it has continued across the centuries. And increasingly we can see that everything in creation has the potential for mediating a word of God to us. Intuition, reason, imagination, reflection, and receptivity — all are tools of the soul that can help us receive the communication of God.

Catherine of Siena
1347-1380

Catherine of Siena was born in 1347 to a very large family — the twenty-fourth of twenty-five children. Her father was a dyer of wool, and her mother, the daughter of a local poet. As a child, Catherine was imaginative and idealistic, outgoing and winsome — and began seeing visions. Already at age seven she consecrated her virginity to Christ, and at sixteen she took vows in the Dominican order. The shaping of Catherine's life may seem strange to us, but we must see her in the context of a world strongly attracted to the monastic ideal.

Her life was short — she lived to be only thirty-three — but very

12. Thomas Aquinas, cited by Donald Nicholl in *Holiness* (New York: Paulist Press, 1981), p. 130.

full. And her devotion to God was balanced between contemplation and action. She tended the sick, served the poor, and worked to convert sinners. Following the summer of 1370, after receiving a series of visions culminating in a divine directive to participate more fully in public life, she began writing letters to men and women in every station of life, including the princes of Italy and papal legates. During this time she played a significant role in returning the papacy from Avignon to Rome.

It's truly remarkable how much public work she was able to do, given the demanding depth of her spiritual life. While in Pisa, she received the stigmata. She also had numerous ecstatic experiences during which her body appeared dead. And it is said that she dictated most of her classic mystical book *The Dialogue* while in a state of ecstasy. One account says that she wrote this book in a five-day period; more probably it took about a year.

The Dialogue is a series of petitions made by Catherine and answered by God. In the opening pages of the book, Catherine makes four requests of the Lord: the first petition is for herself; the second is for the reform of the holy church; the third is for the world in general and also specifically for the peace of Christians who are rebelling against the holy church; and the fourth is for divine providence, both in general and in a particular case. These four requests are then answered one by one.

As books go, this one is quite unusual: God speaks in the first person to Catherine. If we look at excerpts from several key passages, we will get a clear sense of her experience and her message. Take, for example, what God says about "the way":

> "Here is the way, if you would come to perfect knowledge and enjoyment of me, to eternal Life: Never leave the knowledge of yourself. Then, put down as you are in the valley of humility, you will know me in yourself, and from this knowledge you will draw all that you need."[13]

---

13. *Catherine of Siena: The Dialogue,* edited by Suzanne Noffke, O.P. (New York: Paulist Press, 1980), p. 29.

Then there is the vivid description of "the bridge":

> "I want to describe the bridge for you. I have told you that it
> stretches from heaven to earth by reason of my having joined my-
> self with your humanity, which I formed from the earth's clay.
>
> "This bridge, my only-begotten Son, has three stairs. . . . You
> will recognize in these three stairs three spiritual stages.
>
> "The first stair is the feet, which symbolize the affections.
> For just as the feet carry the body, the affections carry the soul.
> My Son's nailed feet are a stair by which you can climb to his side,
> where you will see revealed his inmost heart. For when the soul
> has climbed up on the feet of affection and looked with her
> mind's eye into my Son's open heart, she begins to feel the love of
> her own heart in his consummate and unspeakable love. So, hav-
> ing climbed the second stair, she reaches the third. This is his
> mouth, where she finds peace from the terrible war she has had
> to wage because of her sins."[14]

And there is the description — particularly relevant to our purposes
here — of how God shows himself:

> "The First is my showing of my love and affection in the person of
> the Word, my Son, through his blood poured out in such burning
> love. Beyond the knowledge of ordinary love, these [those who
> have been made God's friends] taste it and know it and experi-
> ence it and feel it in their very souls.
>
> "Love's second showing is simply in souls themselves, when I
> show myself to them in loving affection. [God shows himself to
> those who most earnestly seek, and sometimes God gives the
> Spirit of Prophecy to show them what lies ahead. This can take
> many forms, depending upon what the person needs.]
>
> "At other times . . . I will make them aware of the presence of
> my Truth, my only-begotten Son, and this in different ways, ac-

14. *Catherine of Siena*, pp. 64-65.

cording to their hunger and their will. Sometimes they seek in prayer and want to know power, and I satisfy them by letting them feel my strength. Sometimes they want the wisdom of my Son, and I satisfy them by setting him before their mind's eye."[15]

Even though the intervening years may have romanticized Catherine's experience, it still stands as an uncommon and remarkable revelation of God. These quotations from *The Dialogue* reveal true depth of insight into the ways of God. Although this wisdom came to Catherine while she was in a state of ecstasy, there is nothing nonsensical about what she heard. Obviously, she heard God speak in the context of her social, intellectual, and spiritual environment, but who can doubt the wisdom and integrity of what she has written? Catherine's experience clearly shows that God continued to speak to individuals beyond biblical times.

Julian of Norwich
c. 1342-1416

We know very little about Julian's birth or her life. She lived as a recluse in Norwich, England. When she was thirty years old, she experienced a series of visions during a severe illness. She was so ill that she thought she was dying. She lost feeling in the lower half of her body, then in the upper half. A priest came and showed her a cross, and the room seemed to be filled with darkness except for the cross. Miraculously, Julian recovered, and she wrote of that experience, "And suddenly in that moment all my pain left me, and I was as sound, particularly in the upper part of my body, as ever I was before or have been since."[16]

Subsequently, Julian also wrote about the "showings" she received — first in a brief account and then, two decades later, in a longer, more

---

15. *Catherine of Siena,* p. 116.

16. Julian of Norwich, *Showings: The Short Text,* translated and introduced by Edmund Colledge, O.S.A., and James Walsh, S.J., with a preface by Jean Leclercq, O.S.B. (New York: Paulist Press, 1981), p. 128.

theologically nuanced account. The larger text is indeed rich, but a brief look at the shorter text can give us a vivid picture of her relationship with God.

In the preface to the edition of *Showings* edited by Edmund Colledge and James Walsh, Jean Leclercq describes Julian as a mystic who carefully reflected on her mystical experiences and then logically deduced their meaning. Leclercq says,

> She gets "suggestions" and "sharings"; she then has "doubts." She studiously asks "questions"; finally, she accepts. She consents and "chooses." "Bodily visions" and "corporeal sights" stimulate her search for understanding. The "revelation" is never sufficient; it is a grace, and God takes all the initiative, but includes a place for her own efforts. The extraordinary does not dispense with the ordinary. She chooses the way of asceticism, reflection, study, and humble, daily prayer.[17]

Leclercq further affirms the witness of Julian when he says, "Through her experience and her understanding, she grasps the total mystery of God, as far as this is possible in this life, and she wants to communicate to us a glimpse of it."[18]

Leclercq's assessment fully recognizes the spirit of Julian's work — a spirit we see wonderfully displayed in Julian's description of her vision of Christ's passion:

> I never wanted any bodily vision or any kind of revelation from God, but only the compassion which I thought a loving soul could have for our Lord Jesus, who for love was willing to become a mortal man. I desired to suffer with him, living in my mortal body, as God would give me grace. And at this suddenly I saw the red blood trickling down from under the crown, all hot, flowing freely and copiously, a living stream, just as it seemed to

17. Leclercq, preface to Julian of Norwich, *Showings,* p. 5.
18. Leclercq, preface to Julian of Norwich, *Showings,* p. 11.

me that I was at the time when the crown of thorns was thrust down upon his blessed head. Just so did he, both God and man, suffer for me. I perceived, truly and powerfully, that it was himself who showed this to me, without any intermediary; and then I said: Blessed be the Lord![19]

The Lord clearly showed Julian his love. She saw that she was clothed in love, enfolded, embraced, and guided in love. "And so in this sight I saw truly that he is everything which is good, as I understand."[20]

Julian also saw the depth of the Lord's love in a now-famous "showing" involving an object the size of a hazelnut:

And in this he showed me something small, no bigger than a hazelnut, lying in the palm of my hand, and I perceived that it was as round as any ball. I looked at it and thought: What can this be? And I was given this general answer: It is everything, which is made. I was amazed that it could last, for I thought that it was so little that it could suddenly fall into nothing. And I was answered in my understanding: It lasts and always will, because God loves it; and thus everything has being through the love of God.[21]

"After this," she says, "I saw God in an instant of time, that is, in my understanding, and by this vision I saw that he is present in all things. I contemplated it carefully, knowing and perceiving through it that he does everything which is done."[22]

This small sampling of Julian's descriptions of the "showings" she received vividly illustrates God's manner of speech to her. To her searching soul, God chose to manifest Godself in visions — for the most part, she was seeing rather than hearing.

In the first "showing" excerpted here, Julian speaks of Christ's pas-

19. Julian of Norwich, *Showings*, p. 129.
20. Julian of Norwich, *Showings*, p. 130.
21. Julian of Norwich, *Showings*, pp. 130-31.
22. Julian of Norwich, *Showings*, p. 137.

sion being revealed to her "without any intermediary." Subsequently, however, she does receive God's word through a medium. She has a vision of an object as tiny as a hazelnut in her hand, something small and firm and round. When she asks what it is, she receives a short but comprehensive answer: "It is everything, which is made." This was followed by a short burst of insight that Saint Teresa would call "an intellectual vision." This small object contained a huge revelation: "It lasts and always will, because God loves it; and thus everything has being through the love of God." In this experience we see how God uses a small piece of the creation to speak eternal truths about the whole creation.

Clearly, Julian's visions are a form of GodSpeech that still speaks powerfully to us today.

The individuals highlighted in this chapter provide extraordinary examples of how God continues to speak through the ages. In the next chapter we will look at several more individuals blessed by GodSpeech.

QUESTIONS FOR REFLECTION AND DISCUSSION
1. What are the different ways in which God spoke to the people described in this chapter?
2. Why did Polycarp, Anthony, and Francis make such radical decisions?
3. What is the relationship between these dedicated individuals and the life of the church?
4. What benefits do you personally derive from the experiences of these devout souls?

A SUGGESTION FOR JOURNALING
1. Choose one of the people described in this chapter. Imagine that you are this saint, and based on the brief sketch provided here, write a first-person account of your experience of hearing God speak.

CHAPTER FIVE

GodSpeech: From Teresa of Ávila to Henri Nouwen

The voice of the LORD *flashes forth flames of fire.*

Psalm 29:7

The amazing revelation of God to those who believe continues in an unbroken stream throughout history. Although I have not mentioned individuals like Martin Luther, John Wesley, and Nikolaus Ludwig von Zinzendorf, these stalwarts of the faith truly stand in the line of witnesses to "the God who speaks." Ignatius of Loyola also bears testimony to hearing the voice of God, especially through the stories of Jesus, and he has given us many insights into the discernment of GodSpeech. But I have chosen to continue this line of witnesses by pointing to Teresa of Ávila, George Fox, two anonymous witnesses, and Henri Nouwen. They bring additional insight to the discoveries that we have already made through other witnesses like Polycarp, Anthony of the Desert, Francis of Assisi, Thomas Aquinas, Catherine of Siena, and Julian of Norwich.

Teresa of Ávila
1515-1582

The fourteenth, fifteenth, and sixteenth centuries were a period of great renewal in the Spirit, a time when God manifested Godself in speech to numerous serious disciples. The ferment of the Spirit that erupted in both individuals and movements is evident in both the Catholic Church and the Protestant Church. Names like Martin Luther, John Calvin, and Ulrich Zwingli immediately come to mind when we think of the Protestant expression of church renewal. But in the Catholic Church the names of Ignatius, John of the Cross, and Teresa of Ávila — the Spanish mystics — first come to mind as those most influential in writing about the inner life of people who listen for God.

God spoke to Martin Luther, a troubled monk, in the words of Saint Paul: "The just shall live by faith." This conviction fueled the Reformation that Luther birthed. Luther inspired Calvin with his new understanding of faith. Zwingli and the leaders of the radical wing of the Reformation in Switzerland were also fueled by the same dynamic power that propelled the awakening in France and Germany.

While I could have selected representatives from either of these branches of the Reformation, I have chosen to illustrate GodSpeech in the sixteenth century with Teresa of Ávila, in part because she was so open and vulnerable in her experiences with God, and in part because there is such a wealth of experience in her biography and other writings.

Teresa was born on March 28, 1515, in Ávila, Spain. She was the daughter of a wealthy merchant who was also a devout man. Even as a young child, Teresa showed signs of a deep spiritual sensitivity. She was greatly affected by stories of the lives of the saints and martyrs. She was enthralled by their eagerness to enter into the presence of God as soon as possible — so enthralled, in fact, that when she was just seven years old, she left home with her older brother, wanting to join in fighting the Moors, hoping to be beheaded for Christ's sake. Fortunately, her uncle intercepted the two siblings as they were leaving the city and returned them to their father.

Later in life she recalled her great estimation of the martyrs: "When I read of the martyrdom they suffered for the love of God, I used to think it a very cheap price to pay for their entry into God's presence. Then I fervently longed to die like them, not from any conscious love for him, but so that I might come to enjoy as quickly as they those great joys which I had read are laid up in heaven."[1]

When Teresa was about twenty, she entered the Carmelite Monastery of the Incarnation in Ávila. Early in her experience as a nun, she experienced long periods of infused prayer — a form of prayer in which the pray-er enters into a trancelike state in deep communion with God. During these times she appeared to be dead. Her fellow sisters observed her, and while some were deeply impressed with her piety, others criticized her, claiming that she was seeking to be a saint. These harsh judgments pained Teresa, but she said nothing.

Then one day while she was praying she experienced her first locution (the voice of God speaking in her head): "Do not fret about this, but serve me." These words gave her great consolation. Stephen Clissold, one of her biographers, comments, "The locutions communicated themselves as silently uttered 'inner voices,' directing her in things great and small, instructing her to do this or refrain from doing that, warning, encouraging, occasionally rebuking." She was certain that they were more than her own unconscious desires because "they ran counter to her rational intentions."[2]

Her confessors did not understand her spiritual sensitivity and her special experiences of God. They often advised her to distract herself from God — the very thing that she most desired. She knew they often judged her wrongly and gave her poor direction, but she followed it because she placed obedience to their guidance above her own will and judgment. To encourage her, the inner voice spoke to her again: "Do not be distressed, for I will give you a living book."

She describes how that "living book" — Christ — came to her:

---

1. Quoted by Stephen Clissold in *St. Teresa of Avila* (New York: Seabury Press, 1982), p. 14.

2. Clissold, *St. Teresa of Avila,* p. 44.

When I was praying one day — it was the feast of the glorious St. Peter — I saw Christ beside me, or more exactly, I felt him to be at my side, for I saw nothing with the eyes of the body, neither with those of the soul. But Christ seemed to be close beside me, and I saw that it was he who seemed to be speaking to me. As I was utterly ignorant that such visions were possible, I was very frightened and at first could do nothing but weep. But as soon as he spoke to me, I regained my usual composure and became calm, happy, and quite free from fear. There at my side, so it seemed to me, Jesus Christ stayed, but as this was not an imaginary vision [i.e., a vision involving images], I was unable to see in what form; but that he was all the time at my right and witnessed everything I was doing I most clearly felt.[3]

Fellow pilgrim, do you see in Teresa one who is conversant in GodSpeech? She understood the language of vision, of locution, and of intuition. It is she who has written about the life of the Spirit with the greatest clarity and the deepest insight. Interestingly, it was her superiors who commanded her to write; it was not a vocation she would have chosen. And what rich fruit came of following that directive: *The Way of Perfection, The Interior Castle, Spiritual Relations: Exclamations of the Soul to God,* and *Conceptions on the Love of God,* among others.

Perhaps Teresa's example of obedience should be emphasized for a generation that is fixated on having its own way. Although she knew that her advisors did not understand her experiences of God, she followed their guidance with humility. How many of us would do the same?

George Fox
1624-1691

Perhaps no one else in the history of Christianity has placed more emphasis on the inward experience of Christ than George Fox. Born in Leicestershire in 1624, not too many years after the English Reforma-

---

3. Quoted by Clissold in *St. Teresa of Avila,* p. 53.

tion began, he found himself in a highly liturgical culture with little emphasis on the practice of Christian faith. His parents, about whom he speaks little, were godly people and set good examples, but the kind of faith he saw displayed in his early years had no appeal for him.

As a young man he had a profound hunger for the experience of God, and he set out to discover the meaning of the faith and how he could know and experience the reality of God. He went first to his own pastor to consult with him about the things of God. But the pastor began referring to their conversations in his sermons, and this betrayal of trust forced Fox to look elsewhere for spiritual guidance. At the age of eighteen he became a spiritual vagabond, wandering and wondering from place to place, searching for answers to his questions.

In all his wanderings he got very little help from the pastors he consulted. The first pastor he met with suggested that he sing psalms and take a little tobacco. Like his own pastor, this man revealed Fox's confessions to others — in this case, to his own servants — thus deeply grieving him. Fox referred to the third priest he encountered as "an empty hollow cask" — no help there! The fourth experience was also disastrous. While walking with this priest in his garden, Fox accidentally stepped into a flowerbed, and the priest flew into a rage and verbally abused his young counselee. His hypocrisy saddened Fox. The last spiritual guide Fox consulted suggested that he would benefit from "a physic" and blood-letting — again, no real help was offered. All these pseudo-efforts at spiritual guidance left Fox sorrowful and unfulfilled.[4]

These disappointments provided the awkward context in which the Word of the Lord first came to him. Fox says, "At another time, as I was walking in a field on a First-day morning, the Lord opened unto me that being bred at Oxford or Cambridge was not enough to fit and qualify men to be ministers of Christ; and I stranged at it because it was the common belief of people."[5] If he could not count on the ministers of his

---

4. Fox's experiences are recounted by Eugene Peterson in *Working the Angles: The Shape of Pastoral Integrity* (Grand Rapids: Eerdmans, 1987), pp. 122-27.

5. Fox, *Journal*, cited in *The Quaker Reader* (Wallingford, Pa.: Pendle Hill Publications, 1962), p. 44.

day, and if the schools that they attended could be of no help, where could he turn?

Subsequently, when he had had a particularly difficult experience, another revelation came to him. He heard a voice that said, "There is one, even Christ Jesus, that can speak to thy condition."[6] This encounter with the Voice proved to be a turning point for Fox. He now had a way — the Way — to seek to experience the presence of God.

This experience of Christ's voice speaking to him may also have convinced him that he did not need another to teach him, especially since he had had such disastrous experiences with relogous instruction in the past. His relatives still wanted him to speak to someone for guidance. But to them Fox said, "Did not the apostle say to believers that they needed no man to teach them, but that the anointing [i.e., the Spirit of Christ in them] teaches them?"[7] But how would Christ teach him and all those who believe?

The opening verses of John's Gospel provided the key. In John 1:9 Fox read, "He was the true light that lights every person who comes into the world." This single affirmation opened up to him a "creation spirituality" long before it was in vogue. The Apostle John's witness convinced him that every human being has been touched by the Spirit and that something of the divine remains in each individual. To know the way of God, people must listen to the inner voice and walk in its light. This understanding suggested a phrase often used by Fox — "that of God in every man."

Fox wrote about "the light of Christ in every person" in his journal, which was subsequently published. This conviction was also the guiding principle of the group he founded: the Society of Friends — the Quakers. Fox frequently referred to "the Light within," which shines to illuminate truth in the heart of every individual. It is more than conscience; it is Christ in every person. In addition to "the Light," Fox often spoke of "showings," as in "The Lord showed me . . ." I take this phrasing to

---

6. Fox, *Journal*, cited by Jim Pym in *Listening to the Light* (London: Rider, 1999), p. 25.

7. Fox, *Journal*, cited in *The Quaker Reader*, p. 45.

mean that the inner light shone in his mind, illuminating ideas and reinforcing the truth of convictions. Fox took these "showings" to be the activity of the Spirit of Christ. After pursuing this way for a while, Fox could say, "My desires after the Lord grew stronger, and zeal in the pure knowledge of God and of Christ alone, without the help of any man, book, or writing."[8]

A life of receptive listening drew as much reaction in Fox's day as it would in our own. The priests and magistrates before whom he appeared accused him of exalting himself above the priests, the church, and the Scriptures. His radical approach to the gospel was indeed deemed heresy, and church leaders feared that a reactionary like him would lead people into hideous errors. Consequently, they rejected him and persecuted those who followed him.

Although many in our day would experience the same fears about such an unusual individual, I wonder if we too quickly discount Fox's words and vision. Fear too easily blinds us to the important elements in Christianity that Fox sought to recover. Is it not true that the core of the Hebrew tradition arose from the speech of God to Abraham? Is it not true that Christ is the Word of God spoken to us all? Are we overlooking the testimony of Saint John that Christ enlightens every person who comes into the world? Have we forgotten that Christ's message came to people like us? Have we too easily substituted speech *about* God for the speech *of* God? And finally, have we stopped believing that the God who spoke in the past still speaks today?

Perhaps George Fox and the Quakers have much to teach us about listening to the contemporary speech of God.

The Two Listeners
1930s

When I was a freshman in college, a book fell into my hands that ever since that time has influenced the way I have prayed, listened to God,

8. Fox, *Journal,* cited in *The Quaker Reader,* p. 47.

and lived my life. The name of the book is *God Calling,* and it was edited by A. J. Russell, himself a writer of many inspirational books. It was written by two ordinary women who were well-acquainted with the troubles and sorrows of life.

In the introduction, Russell explained that the two women who wrote the book sought no praise and wanted to remain anonymous — hence "the two listeners." These women made the astonishing claim that the message given to them was from the living Christ himself. "Having read their book," Russell said, "I believe them."

One of the listeners offers insight into the manner and motive for writing as they did. In the fall of 1932, she was sitting in the lounge of a hotel when another hotel visitor approached her. The woman showed her a copy of *For Sinners Only* by A. J. Russell. The stranger asked if she had read the book, and when she said no, the stranger gave it to her.

The woman who received the unexpected gift read the book carefully and was so affected by it that she wanted to give all her friends a copy. She made a list of a hundred people with whom she wished to share the book, but since she was poor, she could only afford two copies.

A few months later she reread the book and wanted to see if she could receive spiritual guidance in the manner that Russell described. She sat down with pencil and paper in hand and listened for God's voice. Try as she might, nothing came to her. She struggled to keep her wandering mind focused, but to no avail. Her efforts got her nowhere.

At the time she was living with a friend, a deeply spiritual woman who was being severely tested but continued to trust God's goodness and willingness to answer prayer. Wanting to try to follow Russell's suggestions again, she asked her friend if she would be willing to join her in "listening sessions" every day. The friend agreed, and the two of them sat together every day in silence, listening for the Lord. Wonderful things began to happen. From the very first session, the Lord spoke to them. Day after day, penetrating and revealing messages came to them. Both of them were amazed. They felt unworthy and overwhelmed when they realized that the Lord himself was teaching, training, and encouraging them so that they might participate in his mission to the world.

Why had he chosen them? Why was he teaching them personally when others went to church, consulted with pastors, and attended school for such training?

These two women did not think of themselves as psychic or advanced in their spirituality; they considered themselves very ordinary people who had known more suffering and worry than most. The words Christ spoke to them brought both chastening and encouragement, but his corrections never caused them pain, and his encouragement always sustained them.

"Always, and this daily, he insisted that we should be channels of love, joy, and laughter in his broken world," they wrote.[9] Those words served as their commission. They found this command both strange and difficult, considering their circumstances. How could they laugh, cheer others on, and be joyful continuously when their days were pain-racked and their nights tortured by chronic insomnia, when poverty and insurmountable worry were their daily portion? How could they be positive in thought and filled with cheery hope when their prayers for healing went unanswered and clouds of doubt covered God's face every day? Without the mutual support they gave each other, doubtless they would have ceased their listening, but with God's strength and Christ's daily administrations of grace, they persevered. As a consequence, we have a book that testifies to the God who speaks.

In the reading for January 1 in *God Calling,* the Lord speaks:

> Dwell not on the past — only on the present. Only use the past as the trees use my Sunlight, to absorb it, to make from it in after days the warming fire-rays. So store only the blessings from me, the Light of the World. Encourage yourselves by the thought of these. Bury every fear of the future, of poverty for those dear to you, of suffering, of loss. Bury all thought of unkindness and bitterness, all your dislikes, your resentments, your sense of failure, your disappointment in others and in yourselves, your gloom,

9. *God Calling,* ed. A. J. Russell (Uhrichsville, Ohio: Barbour Publishing, Inc., 1993), p. 10.

your despondency, and let us leave them all, buried, and go forward to a new and risen life.[10]

The reading for March 29 is as follows:

> I reward your seeking with my presence. Rejoice and be glad.
> I am your God. Courage and joy will conquer all troubles. First things first.
> Seek me, love me, joy in me. I am your Guide. No perils can affright you, no discipline exhaust you. Persevere. Can you hold on in my strength? I need you more than you need me. Struggle through this time for my sake. Initiation precedes all real work and success for me.

The GodSpeech for July 17 reads, "Rejoice, rejoice. I have much to teach you both. Think not that I withhold my presence when I do not reveal more of my truth to you. You are passing through a storm. Enough that I am with you to say, 'Peace, be still,' to quiet both winds and waves. It was on the quiet mountain slopes that I taught my disciples the truths of my kingdom, not during the storm. So with you, the time of the mountain slopes will come, and you shall rest with me and learn."

In the midst of their poverty and pain, these gallant souls took time each day to receive God's instruction. God did not disappoint them, and because of their faithfulness, we have a treasury of wisdom, insight, and encouragement.

Most of the hearers of GodSpeech that I have focused on thus far are persons of note in the life of the church; many are shapers of the world. The "two listeners" in *God Calling* are ordinary people struggling through life, like most of us. Unfortunately, we do not possess a record of the myriad witnesses of unknown saints who have listened for Christ to speak and have heard and obeyed — although they are certainly known to God. But the testimony of these two lesser-known

---

10. Since the book does not have page numbers, I refer to the quotations by the days of the year.

saints shows that God is willing to speak "to the least of us," if we are willing to listen for the Voice.

This daring experiment took place in the early twentieth century, perhaps suggesting to us that the God who spoke to Abraham was still speaking less than a century ago.

Henri Nouwen
1932-1996

In the last half of the twentieth century, no spiritual writer provided more inspiration, offered greater guidance, or exerted more influence in the field of spirituality than Henri Nouwen. He wrote numerous books, taught in seminaries, and gave lectures around the world. He grew from experiences of God in diverse settings: a monastery on the Genesee River; life amid the poor in South America; the faculties of America's most distinguished universities; a haven for the mentally handicapped. All these experiences molded his life and found their way into his writing.

Of all the books he wrote, none demonstrates the speech of God more simply and naturally than one published after his death, *The Inner Voice of Love*. Nouwen never intended to publish this book; it was a series of imperatives he wrote to himself. The occasion for the writing of these bluntly stated directives arose from the spiritual desolation he experienced between December 1987 and June 1988. This was a period of extreme anguish, during which his life came apart. He says, "Everything came crashing down — my self-esteem, my energy to live and work, my sense of being loved, my hope for healing, my trust in God . . . everything."[11] During this time, the man who had been the great spiritual leader experienced the depths of human misery and abandonment; he felt as if God had left him, as if the home of his soul had no floors. He could not sleep. He cried for hours. Words of love and consolation could not reach him.

---

11. Nouwen, *The Inner Voice of Love* (New York: Image Books, 1996), p. xiii.

This crisis, which seemed more than he could bear, was precipitated by the loss of a significant relationship. With his life in shambles and his sense of himself shattered, he turned to people that he hoped could lead him to a new freedom and wholeness. Although during this period he lost his love for music and his appreciation for the beauty of nature and art, he never lost his ability to write. So each day after his appointment with his two spiritual guides, he wrote a "spiritual imperative" that came out of the session.

Nouwen insisted that he wrote these imperatives for himself alone, but they were clearly more than that, and both his friends and his publisher prevailed upon him to publish them. Nouwen says these directives came from his own mind, but when I read them, I got the keen sense that he was not only talking to himself but also being "spoken through." God spoke through his pain and emptiness to the pain and emptiness in all of us. The title of the book — *The Inner Voice of Love* — also suggests that the words arose in him but originated from beyond him. I believe it was the voice of the Spirit speaking to him, perhaps using his pain and the guidance given him by his two spiritual counselors.

When I first read this book, I realized that Christ spoke through Nouwen's pain to my own. And then I remembered two friends of mine who were also going through a great deal of pain. They seemed unable to shake it. It clung to their souls and claimed their every waking moment. The homes of their souls had no floors, either. I copied some selections from Nouwen's book and sent them to my two friends for their consolation. These selections — some of which I'm including below — illustrate why I believe the Spirit inspired the words Nouwen wrote as directives for us all. Here, in another circumstance and in a completely different manner, we have the same phenomenon that we discovered in Saint Teresa, "the two listeners," and George Fox — the voice of God speaking to the human spirit. When you read what follows, you will know what I mean:

Conversion is certainly not something you can bring about yourself. It is not a question of willpower. You have to trust the inner voice that shows the way. You know that inner voice. You turn to it often.[12]

There are two realities to which you must cling. First, God has promised that you will receive the love for which you have been searching. And, second, God is faithful to that promise.[13]

You complain that it is hard for you to pray, to experience the love of Jesus. But Jesus dwells in your fearful, never fully received self. When you befriend your true self and discover that it is good and beautiful, you will see Jesus there. Where you are most human, most yourself, weakest, there Jesus lives. Bringing your fearful self home is bringing Jesus home.[14]

Be patient and trust. You have to move gradually deeper into your heart. There is a place far down that is like a turbulent river, and that place frightens you. But do not fear. One day it will be quiet and peaceful.[15]

It is not going to be easy to listen to God's call. Your insecurity, your self-doubt, and your great need for affirmation make you lose trust in your inner voice and run away from yourself. But you know that God speaks to you through your inner voice and that you will find joy and peace only if you follow it. Yes, your spirit is willing to follow, but your flesh is weak.[16]

The root choice is to trust at all times that God is with you and will give you what you most need. Your self-rejecting emotions might say, "It isn't going to work. I'm still suffering the same anguish I did six months ago. I will probably fall back into the old

12. Nouwen, *The Inner Voice of Love*, p. 6.
13. Nouwen, *The Inner Voice of Love*, p. 12.
14. Nouwen, *The Inner Voice of Love*, p. 49.
15. Nouwen, *The Inner Voice of Love*, p. 55.
16. Nouwen, *The Inner Voice of Love*, p. 89.

depressive patterns of acting and reacting. I haven't really changed." And on and on. It is hard not to listen to these voices. Still you know that these are not God's voice. God says to you, "I love you. I am with you. I want to see you come closer to me and experience the joy and peace of my presence. I want to give you a new heart and a new spirit. I want you to speak with my mouth, see with my eyes, hear with my ears, and touch with my hands. All that is mine is yours. Just trust me and let me be your God." This is the voice to listen to. And that listening requires a real choice, not just once in a while but every moment of each day and night.[17]

The morning after I had sent off these selections to my dear friends, while I was praying for them, I had a vision. I don't know whether it was a self-induced projection of my desire or a true gift from God. Even if it was a creation of my own mind, I think the Spirit was a part of it in some fashion.

In the vision, the screen of my mind was dark blue, and then washes of black began to pour across the landscape. The blueness fought against the blackness, and gradually the blueness began to win and turn lighter and lighter.

As the screen of my imagination turned light blue, my two friends walked out onto the stage with their backs to me. They stood with their arms hanging loosely by their sides, staring upward. I strained to see what they were looking at but could not glimpse it. Then it came to me: they were looking up into the balcony of heaven, where the prophets, the saints, the mystics, and the martyrs — the whole family of God — was watching them struggle and cheering them on.

They were not alone in this battle for their souls! The Voice speaking in Nouwen would also speak to them. The voice of God that spoke through the ages longed to give them encouragement and strength, just as God had strengthened "the two listeners."

17. Nouwen, *The Inner Voice of Love,* pp. 113-14.

And All the Others

In the last half of the twentieth century, North America — and to some extent the Western world — has been experiencing a longing to hear "the God who speaks." In response to this yearning, numerous contemplatives, mystics, and writers have arisen, offering guidance in this quest. To attempt a complete listing of contemporary spiritual writers would be futile, but to illustrate the point, I will name a number who have been instructive to me.

My list of helpful and influential speakers and writers includes Evelyn Underhill, Andrew Murray, Douglas V. Steere, Thomas Merton, Henri Nouwen, Elton Trueblood, Frank Laubach, Agnes Sanford, Glen Clark, Thomas Kelly, C. S. Lewis, Glen Hinson, Richard Foster, Dallas Willard, Walter Wink, Carlo Carretto, Reuben Job, Walter Brueggemann, James Fenhagen, Tilden Edwards, Urban T. Holmes, Parker Palmer, Eugene Peterson, Scott Peck, Robert Moore, Morton Kelsey, Kenneth Leech, Thomas H. Green, Susan Muto, Adrian Van Kaam, Julie Johnson, Brad Kent, Charles Olsen, and Anthony de Mello.

Is this not enough, my pilgrim companions, to establish the fact that God still speaks? This selective review of twenty centuries surely gives ample evidence of the continuous experience of GodSpeech among the people of God. It has come to us through diverse people and through numerous movements, but always with amazing power and clarity. Always in times of spiritual crisis there arise leaders to show the way to the blind and to awaken the people of God to their heritage.

For too long the people of God have lived on a memory of a memory — the memory of what others remembered. That secondhand communion can be surpassed. We ourselves can listen to God!

QUESTIONS FOR REFLECTION AND DISCUSSION
1. What contribution does each of the people discussed here make to our understanding of the manner in which God speaks?
2. What evidence do you see in Saint Teresa that she is not delusional but truly inspired by the Spirit?

3. What is your estimate of "the two listeners"? Which quotation seems especially helpful to you?
4. How do you think Nouwen's crisis of darkness relates to the speech of God?

A SUGGESTION FOR JOURNALING

Imagine that you are each of the individuals described in this chapter. Choose an experience of one of them and relate it as though it happened to you.

Practical Applications

CHAPTER SIX

The Practice of Prayer
as Response to GodSpeech

The voice of the LORD *shakes the wilderness; the* LORD *shakes the wilderness of Kadesh.*

Psalm 29:8

The vignettes and the testimonies of women and men who have heard the speech of God could be extended indefinitely. The biographical sketches I have provided of a dozen or so notables merely hint at the veracity and continuity of GodSpeech in its multiple forms, settings, and personalities. The broad spaces of time and experience that separate the spiritual leaders I have focused on could be filled with hundreds of thousands of persons who have listened to and responded to God — if only we knew their names. These unknown saints who have lived in communion with God are as valuable as the deeply devout who are famous. Those who have heard God speak to them in one or more of the myriad forms God chooses range from high to low, rich to poor, sovereign to slave, famous to unknown. So vast are the masses of those who have responded to the voice of God that we could never recount them all.

Learning Primary Speech

I have labeled the direct address of God "primary GodSpeech," but this divine speech does not encompass the whole of primary speech. Obviously, primary GodSpeech points to God's speech to us, but our speech to God is also primary speech. I can imagine no human speech more basic than simple words and cries directed to God. Others have also recognized the primal nature of this response to God. From the pagan to the saint, all speak the language of prayer — believer and unbeliever alike. When the happenings of our lives evoke these primal cries, to whom are they directed?

I believe they are addressed to God, whether the pray-er knows it or not. These pleas or praises rise to whomever the bursting soul knows as God. And these overflowing expressions of the soul, no matter how self-generated they seem, are inspired by the Spirit. Yes, it is God who teaches us to speak in response. Can you not picture these moments of instruction given by God? When God draws near, God's very presence evokes a response of primal prayer.

The old instruction spoken to children seems to apply: "Speak when you are spoken to." Most often this directive keeps children silent and does not allow them to participate in adult conversations. They understand that they are not to speak until an adult invites them into the conversation. This instruction reminds us also of another primal image: that of a parent or grandparent teaching a child to speak. Hearing and absorbing language is what allows a child to speak. Picture a new mother looking into the eyes of her six-month-old daughter and methodically repeating "Mama, Mama," hoping to hear her child repeat the word. Isn't this primary speech? The first awkward sounds of gurgling or crying, then the first words stimulated by a parent's persistence.

The parent teaching the child to speak illustrates the primary speech of the Heavenly Parent and our primary response. God comes to us in our spiritual infancy and speaks to us in ways that evoke our responses. Like the child uttering "Mama" or "Dada," we may have no idea what our primal sounds mean. Furthermore, we have no idea how these sounds thrill the Teacher; like the parent, our Teacher is also ecstatic upon hearing the sounds coming from our souls.

These primal encounters with God call forth primary responses of prayer and mark the early stages in our learning the language of God. The gracious God teaches us slowly but persistently, as we begin to acquire the vocabulary that enables us to name experiences, express desires, and define more clearly our responses to the coming and going of God in our lives. As we become more proficient in the language of God, our expressions — though not necessarily in words — are fuller, richer, and more encompassing of our experiences.

This paradigm of the parent teaching the child the language of the family or the clan underscores the fact that we cannot speak until we have been spoken to. The speech of God *to us* awakens the speech of God *in us*. Primal speech from God gives birth to primal speech in us. Primal speech is original speech, basic speech, speech that matters, and while preliminary in one way, it is ultimate in another.

The revelation of God in human consciousness — or, as we are calling it, the speech of God — takes the initiative to grasp, shake, and move the human spirit. This movement of the human spirit in its earlier manifestations results from the nature of God as One who comes to us and reveals Godself to us. The revelation of God in human consciousness has the character of mystery, miracle, and ecstasy. The spontaneous response that we make to this incursion of the Spirit is what I mean by primary, responsive speech. God comes to us and speaks; our response is prayer, whether it is made in intelligible words, unintelligible speech, or shouts of joy or wonder.

This notion of primary responsive speech became both clearer and simpler to me when I was speaking with Rose Mary Dougherty of the Shalom Institute. She said that in prayer we should listen for the prayer that Jesus is praying in us. I knew that Jesus lived to make intercession for us, and I knew that we prayed with him to the Father. But it had never before dawned on me that Jesus is making his prayer in us and sometimes through us. Thus it is important to listen to the prayer that Jesus is praying in us. This responsive way of praying might be called secondary speech. I reserve "secondary speech" to describe our speech "about" God rather than our speech to God.

Carlo Carretto also makes the divine initiative in prayer very clear in his book entitled *The God Who Comes*:

> We must assume an attitude of waiting, accepting the fact that we are creatures and not creator. We must do this because it is not our right to do anything else; the initiative is God's, not man's. Man is able to initiate nothing; he is able only to accept. If God does not call, no calling takes place. If God does not come, there is no history! History is the coming of God to man, and the way in which man replies.[1]

Carlo further clarifies God's coming to us when he says, "Between him and me there is always a space, even if only the thickness of the placenta in which I am enfolded like a fetus in his womb. I am I, and He is He. I am son, and He is Father. I am one who waits, and He is the One who comes. I am one who replies, and He is the One who calls."[2] In the encounter we actually feel like we are taking the action, only to realize later that God acted first.

Learning the Hallmarks of Responsive GodSpeech

When God comes to us as mystery, we respond with awe and wonder. When God's steadfast love is revealed to us, we give thanks. When we are confronted with the holiness of God, we can do nothing less than pour out our confession of estrangement and sin. When we feel God's generosity and attentiveness, we offer petitions for his good gifts. When God invites us into the communion of divine love, our sense of sharing in God's work flows outward in prayers of intercession for the whole world. The divine presence in its myriad forms elicits multiple forms of

1. Carretto, *The God Who Comes* (Maryknoll, N.Y.: Orbis Press, 1974), p. 28.
2. Carretto, *The God Who Comes*, p. 29.

prayer in and through us. God's nature disclosed to us not only elicits our prayer but also gives birth to its form.

Just as these different encounters with God teach us different modes of primary GodSpeech, the absence of God also instructs us. We do not go far on the Christian journey before we discover that God does not always appear when we expect, and that God sometimes leaves us in the dark with a fear of being forsaken. Yet through the centuries God's faithful people have learned that God often chooses to be silent to teach us to pray. In darkness, stunned by the silence of God, believers have found ways to groan their prayers when God seemed far away and they themselves were wrapped in sunless clouds.

Attending God's manifestations to us — from deep mystery to deep silence — teaches us the source of every form of prayer. Naming these forms of prayer and the revelation of God that inspires them will ground our prayer in God and will enable us to maintain the connection between God and our prayer, or God's prayer in us.

Mystery

In some sense, every meeting with God contains mystery. God approaches us from the mystery, but also always remains in mystery. Even when God reveals Godself to us, the encounter conceals some other aspect of the divine. No revelation is ever full and complete, so mystery is ever present.

German theologian and philosopher Rudolf Otto leads us into the mystery with a profound biblical exploration of the holy. This holy God comes into human awareness as a tremendous mystery, one that calls for "on your knees" worship and spontaneous praise. We never feel closer to Isaiah's cry of confession than when the Holy One confronts us in mystery.

What do you suppose Abraham felt when God said to him, "I will bless you and make your name great"? He must have thought, "How can it be that this unnamed God will bless me, grant me a land, and make my offspring as numerous as the stars in the heavens and as many as the grains of sand on the seashore?" Imagine the ecstasy that accompanied the anticipation of this promise! Mystery, promise, and ecstasy gave birth to Abraham's primary speech to God.

A primary place to discover human primary speech is in the book of Psalms, the worship book of the Hebrew people. Eugene Peterson speaks of the psalms as "answering God," answering the God who speaks. One of the most consistent responses to God is spontaneous praise. "Praise the LORD! Praise the LORD, O my soul! I will praise the LORD as long as I live; I will sing praises to my God all my life long" (Ps. 146:1-2).

The one who prayed this prayer would agree with Brother Carlo when he says that the wonder and mystery of life lead to prayer: "For is not wonder the first, unconscious meeting with the mystery? Does not wonder give birth to the first prayer? Does not the power to contemplate involve first the power to be awed?"[3] God's mysterious self begets prayers of awe and wonder!

O God, you are mystery. Even when you reveal yourself, you are mystery still. The greatest mystery and my deepest sense of awe arise from Creation. You made me. You gave me the chance to participate in the life of earth and the life of the ages. Hallowed be your Name!

Steadfast Love

The God who comes arrives as love — gracious, steadfast, unfailing love. This love may come in multiple ways and at different times, but it often comes when we are at the end of our strength and wondering if we will survive the night. In that dark moment when we are too weak to reach out, love reaches out to us. In the grasp of love we are empowered to go on, to take the next step, even though the pathway before us has faded in the darkness.[4]

3. Carretto, *The God Who Comes*, p. 6.

4. One woman testifies, "Perhaps the closest I have come to audibly hearing the voice of God was when I was holding my lifeless newborn son in my arms. In that dark moment, I was overwhelmingly convinced of God's presence — and somehow knew that I was being called to accept that as sufficient."

As I recall those times that love has come in the nick of time, a flood of images spontaneously flood my mind: an outstretched hand to guide me in the darkness; a drink of cool water in the heat of summer; a feast of food for my starving soul; and a light shining in the darkness, dissolving my fears.

Israel uttered prayers that spoke to all the circumstances of their life — and still speak to ours. They were certain of the steadfast love of God, no matter how painful the course and how dark the ways they traveled. This is one of their prayers:

> O give thanks to the LORD, for he is good; for his steadfast love endures forever. Let the redeemed of the LORD say so, those he redeemed from trouble and gathered in from the lands, from the east and from the west, from the north and from the south. Some wandered in desert wastes, finding no way to an inhabited town; hungry and thirsty, their soul fainted within them. Then they cried to the LORD in their trouble, and he delivered them from their distress; he led them by a straight way, until they reached an inhabited town. Let them thank the LORD for his steadfast love, for his wonderful works to humankind. For he satisfies the thirsty, and the hungry he fills with good things. (Ps. 107:1-9)

Here the psalmist addresses those whom God saved from physical want, from storm-tossed seas, from darkness and gloom, from sinful ways. He affirms the goodness of God in all these situations, and he urges thanksgiving. He then concludes with these words: "Let those who are wise give heed to these things, and consider the steadfast love of the LORD" (v. 43).

The unsurpassed goodness of God awakens our hearts and shapes on our lips the prayer of thanks.

My Lord, all that I possess is from you. All that I value most is from you! For every gift that you have given, thank you. For every prayer that you have answered, thank you. Thank you most for your lovingkindness and tender mercy.

Holiness

God also comes to us as the Holy One — wholly other, wholly for us, and wholly pure. Holiness, like mystery, grasps the heart and squeezes it until it cries out, confessing its brokenness and alienation. When the Holy Presence manifests itself, the only appropriate response is confession. The God who comes to us in holiness intends not our destruction but our healing, not our exclusion but our acceptance, and to that end comes to us with outstretched arms.[5]

Scripture relates two particularly dramatic encounters with divine holiness. The first instance we read about in Isaiah 6. When Isaiah went to the temple to worship, the Lord appeared to him in a vision with attending seraphim, one crying to the other, "Holy, holy, holy, Lord God of hosts; the whole earth is full of his glory" (v. 3). And Isaiah responded, "Woe is me! I am lost, for I am a man of unclean lips, and I live among a people of unclean lips; yet my eyes have seen the King, the Lord of hosts!" (v. 5). The appearance of holiness led Isaiah to confession, and confession led to purification, symbolized by the live coal with which one of the seraphim touched his lips.

The other encounter with holiness to which I refer occurred not in the temple but in a boat on the lake, an encounter we read about in Luke 5. This transcendent vision of holiness came after the sermon Jesus preached from Peter's boat. When he finished preaching, Jesus instructed Peter to push off into deep water and let down his nets. Having fished all night with no fish to show for it, Peter resisted at first. But when he followed Jesus' suggestion, Peter and his companions caught so many fish that they needed help from their partners in another boat.

In the midst of this strange episode, insight dawned upon Peter! Perhaps he was thinking, "All night we fished these waters and caught nothing. Now, at the direction of this man who is not a fisherman, our boats have been filled to overflowing." It was at this moment that Peter

---

5. A marriage counselor once said to a struggling couple, "God loves us just as we are, Jesus shows us how far we have to go, and the Holy Spirit shows us the path to holiness." We do not find holiness; it finds us — in both joy and pain.

realized that he was dealing with holiness. Like a sharp razor blade, this experience slit the veil between the earthly and the heavenly, between the human and the holy. When the boats, so heavily laden with fish, threatened to sink, Peter fell down at Jesus' knees and cried out, "Go away from me, Lord, for I am a sinful man!" (5:8). Jesus responded with reassurance: "Do not be afraid; from now on you will be catching people" (5:10).

An extraordinary event in an ordinary day opened Peter's eyes to see the holy in the midst of fishing and net-mending. The vision revealed the deepest needs of his life, and a confession fell from his lips. Jesus heard his confession and the request for his departure. Jesus did depart — but with Peter at his side.

In both of these instances, the appearance of the holy led to confession of the true condition of the heart. The experience of the holiness of God correlates directly with this primal speech of confession. This basic form of primary speech has been set forth in numerous forms in the psalms. Probably the best-known confession is Psalm 51, which presumably is that of David after his adultery with Bathsheba and his murder of her husband, Uriah:

> Have mercy on me, O God, according to your steadfast love; according to your abundant mercy blot out my transgressions. Wash me thoroughly from my iniquity, and cleanse me from my sin. For I know my transgressions, and my sin is ever before me. Against you, you alone, have I sinned, and done what is evil in your sight, so that you are justified in your sentence and blameless when you pass judgment. . . . Create in me a clean heart, O God, and put a new and right spirit within me. Do not cast me away from your presence, and do not take your holy spirit from me. Restore to me the joy of your salvation, and sustain in me a willing spirit. (51:1-4, 10-12)

Imagine David going to the temple, and there, amid the smoke rising from the altar in the stillness of this holy place, his troubled soul chokes out a prayer. The guilt of his sin weighs heavily upon him. While waiting in this sacred place, God's holiness touches him, and he cries, "Have mercy!"

To turn away from confession when we stare into God's holiness deepens the paralysis of guilt that clings so tightly and leads to greater alienation and misery. God does not expect us to be perfect, to always know and do the right thing, but God does expect us to acknowledge that his presence reveals truth not only about Godself but also about ourselves. To keep our mouths shut confines us to the dungeon of guilt with its accompanying helplessness. Hear the testimony of one who learned this lesson the hard way:

> While I kept silence, my body wasted away through my groaning all day long. For day and night your hand was heavy upon me; my strength was dried up as by the heat of summer. Then I acknowledged my sin to you, and I did not hide my iniquity; I said, "I will confess my transgressions to the LORD," and you forgave the guilt of my sin. (Ps. 32:3-5)

The holiness of God exposes the depths of our sin and leads us to humble confession.

Without you, O God, I am nothing. I have yearned to live for you, but I have so often fallen short. Forgive and accept me! I have no life, no hope, and no joy apart from you. But in you I have found what I have sought for a lifetime: your self.

Freedom

Withdrawal and Absence The God who made the worlds and sustains them by a word, the God who purposes and brings it to pass, and the God who manifests Godself as mystery, steadfast love, and holiness is also free. God is free for us, but also free from us. We cannot alter God's freedom by our desires, needs, or wishes. Nor can we grasp and hold God in our mind or will. Although in God's freedom God has chosen for us — pro-human — this does not give us control of the divine.

The clear implication of God's freedom for us relates to posture —
open and not grasping. We can be open to the coming of God, we can be
receptive; but we cannot cling to the Presence or control it. Perhaps the
clearest picture of this posture of openness shows itself in Jesus' response to Mary on the morning of his resurrection. He says to her, "Do
not hold on to me, because I have not yet ascended to the Father" (John
20:17). We can never cling to the presence of the living Christ. In his
freedom he comes to us, and in his freedom he may move away from us,
leaving the impression that he no longer walks with us. The hasty departure from the disciples at Emmaus suggests this.

God's freely manifesting Godself to us and then withdrawing the
Presence from us gives birth to prayers of lament. When prayers go unanswered and needs go unmet and we feel forsaken and alone, our disappointment gives birth to complaint.

In the prayer book of the Bible, complaints were frequently filed
with God. By contrast, many devout souls today tend to hold themselves
responsible for God's unresponsiveness. Many, I fear, fail to be honest
with God about their deepest feelings. This difficulty arises when the
tension between God's steadfast love and God's holiness has been broken. If we turn toward God's love and forget God's holiness, we place all
the blame upon God in self-centered pride. On the other hand, when
holiness lacks the tempering of love, we blame God's silence upon ourselves and our sinfulness. Both love and holiness must be held in tension
if we are to be honest about ourselves before God.

Only in recent years have I come to appreciate the psalms of complaint and lament. The tone and content of these prayers came not from
the intimate presence of God but rather from the absence of God and
the resulting emptiness. You may not have experienced the despair
brought about through a sense of God's absence, but if you live long
enough, you probably will.

Henri Nouwen's powerful testimony of his own devastation will either call forth a memory of your own pain or expose you to the possibility that lies before you. In *The Inner Voice of Love,* he writes, "Just when
all those around me were assuring me they loved me, cared for me, ap-
preciated me, yes, even admired me, I experienced myself as a useless,

unloved, and despicable person. Just when people were putting their arms around me, I saw the endless depth of my human misery and felt that there was nothing worth living for. Just when I had found a home, I felt absolutely homeless. Just when I was being praised for my spiritual insights, I felt devoid of faith. Just when people were thanking me for bringing them closer to God, I felt that God had abandoned me. It was as if the house I had finally found had no floors. The anguish completely paralyzed me. I could no longer sleep. I cried uncontrollably for hours. I could not be reached by consoling words or arguments. . . . All had become darkness."[6] Here is a soul seasoned for lament! Here is a confession that names it clearly.

In another setting, the psalmist offered up his lament to God when he found himself in a similar state of the soul:

> I cry aloud to God, aloud to God, that he may hear me. In the day of my trouble I seek the Lord; in the night my hand is stretched out without wearying; my soul refuses to be comforted. I think of God, and I moan; I meditate, and my spirit faints. You keep my eyelids from closing; I am so troubled that I cannot speak. I consider the days of old, and remember the years of long ago. I commune with my heart in the night; I meditate and search my spirit: "Will the Lord spurn forever, and never again be favorable? Has his steadfast love ceased forever? Are his promises at an end for all time? Has God forgotten to be gracious? Has he in anger shut up his compassion?" And I say, "It is my grief that the right hand of the Most High has changed." (Ps. 77:1-10)

In this instance, the psalmist's anguish was assuaged when he recalled the righteous deeds of God.

When "the two listeners" I described in the previous chapter faced the pain in their lives, they heard words of encouragement. Here is what Christ said to them on January 11:

---

6. Nouwen, *The Inner Voice of Love* (New York: Image Books, 1996), pp. xiv-xv.

Life has hurt you. Only scarred lives can really save. You cannot escape the discipline. It is the hallmark of discipleship. My children, trust me always. Never rebel. The trust given to me today takes away the ache of rejection of My Love that I suffered on Earth, and have suffered through the ages. I died for you, My children. How could you treat me so?[7]

The freedom of God that sometimes causes us to experience the pain of abandonment calls forth our lamentations.

O my God, where are you? I have entrusted my soul to you, but I cannot find you. I pray, but my words fall back into my mouth. Please give me eyes to see your presence in the darkness of your absence.

Generosity and Attentiveness   In sharp contrast with the absence of God is God's attentiveness, an awareness of which — thankfully — fills most of our days. Most of the time God expresses his freedom in attentiveness and presence rather than abandonment and absence. In the Old Testament, God is represented as the Creator and Sustainer, as the head of a people loved and cared for. In the New Testament, Jesus teaches us that God is our Father, that God knows all about us and loves each one of us. Jesus clearly instructs us to ask, seek, knock, and to express the deepest desires of our hearts to this One who loves us.

This generosity and attentiveness, the other side of God's freedom, leads us to petition God, to ask for what we desire and to confidently expect God to answer our requests.

Because the psalmist lived in the steadfast love of the Lord, he courageously asked for personal vindication. The Middle Eastern culture in which he lived placed great emphasis on honor and shame. Social status correlated directly with how honorable one was thought to be. The pray-er in Psalm 26 goes to great lengths to establish his integrity, to offer a self-affirming defense that can be made only by one convinced of God's lovingkindness:

7. *God Calling*, ed. A. J. Russell (Uhrichsville, Ohio: Barbour Publishing, Inc., 1993), n.p.

Vindicate me, O LORD, for I have walked in my integrity, and I have rested in the LORD without wavering. Prove me, O LORD, and try me; test my heart and mind. For your steadfast love is before my eyes, and I walk in faithfulness to you. I do not sit with the worthless, nor do I consort with hypocrites; I hate the company of evildoers, and will not sit with the wicked. I wash my hands in innocence, and go around your altar, O LORD. (26:1-6)

Saint Paul also made bold requests of God. He testified that God gave him a thorn in the flesh to help him conquer his pride. Doubtless this thorn was some sort of physical ailment that reminded him of his constant dependence upon God. We do not know the exact nature of this hindrance, but we do know that Paul petitioned the Lord three times for its removal, emboldened by the generosity of Christ. Obviously, the prayer was not answered in the way Paul had expected it to be, because the thorn remained. But the promise Paul did receive underscored to him again the generosity of Christ: "My grace is sufficient for you" (2 Cor. 12:9).

Of those who heard God speak, none illustrated more perfectly the deep, earnest plea for help than Saint Augustine. Persistently he urged God to act in his life, and to act soon. One of these urgent prayers came shortly before his conversion: "How long, how long? Tomorrow and tomorrow? Why not now? Why not in this very hour put an end to my uncleanness?"[8]

Like these well-known petitioners, all of us have made urgent requests in prayer. Close observation reveals a difference between requests that flow out of relative calm and those that come in times of crisis; there is also a difference between prayers of self-centered yearning and prayers sparked by God's generosity. The first often express a blind greediness: my wants and desires above all. But the generosity of God inspires confidence and hope in prayers that are neither demanding nor grasping.

8. *The Confessions of St. Augustine,* translated by John K. Ryan (Garden City, N.Y.: Image Books, 1960), p. 202.

The graciousness of God inspires our petitions. Here is one of mine:

O my gracious God, you have brought me to the closing chapter of my life. I do not know how long it will be, but I do know that all my previous chapters have prepared me for the next phase of the journey. Grant me the spirit of expectancy with which to greet each day, courage to face all the changes, and faith to persevere through the final test.

Community

God comes to us as community because God is eternally Father, Son, and Spirit. Eternally, God has begotten the Son through the Spirit, thus establishing community as the essence of the divine life. In those instances when God comes to us as Father, the Son and the Spirit are always present in the background. Likewise, when the Son speaks to us and within us, the Spirit and the Father are never absent. So it is also when the Spirit is in the foreground.

God comes to us, revealing Godself in all its fullness and inviting us into that communion of divine love. The unconditional love of God embraces all people and all of creation. The desires of this holy community of love become the substance of our prayers. Thus we pray Christ's prayer, "who desires everyone to be saved and to come to the knowledge of the truth" (1 Tim. 2:4). And God wills justice and peace for all people and all nations, a divine desire in which our prayer participates.

The communal nature of God calls forth, inspires, and shapes our prayers of intercession. When, therefore, we pray for others, we participate in God's amazing goodwill for humanity. This God-inspired intercession expresses our confidence in the ultimate intention of God for all life's needs to be met, for justice and peace for all, and for nothing less than human transformation. In short, intercession that participates in the communal nature of God ultimately seeks the Kingdom of God, the ultimate and final community on earth.

At the moment of his death, Jesus turned his compassionate attention toward his followers. He prayed for them. He asked for their pro-

tection and preservation so that they could continue the work he had begun. In making these requests with foresight and vision, he prayed for
all who would believe in him through the witness of his followers. At the
center of this intercession stood the Holy Trinity. This is his prayer:

> As you have sent me into the world, so I have sent them into the
> world. And for their sakes I sanctify myself, so that they also may
> be sanctified in truth. I ask not only on behalf of these, but also
> on behalf of those who will believe in me through their word, that
> they may all be one. As you, Father, are in me and I am in you, may
> they also be in us, so that the world may believe that you have sent
> me.
>
> The glory that you have given me I have given them, so that
> they may be one, as we are one, I in them and you in me, that they
> may become completely one, so that the world may know that
> you have sent me and have loved them even as you have loved me.
> (John 17:18-23)

Through this prayer, Jesus sought to bring every disciple into the life of
the Trinity, his immediate followers and those who would believe in him
through their witness.

Polycarp, the saintly bishop of Smyrna, participated in this communal prayer when he retired to an upper room to spend time in prayer before his arrest. He did not pray to be spared a martyr's death. He did not
even pray for a stay of his execution. Rather, he prayed for the church,
that fledgling collection of Christian gatherings in Asia Minor. He had
been filled with a presence that inspired prayer for the faithful witness
of the church.

In praying this way, Polycarp was simply following in the steps of
his Lord, who, when he was facing his own perilous hour, prayed for his
disciples:

> I am asking on their behalf; I am not asking on behalf of the
> world, but on behalf of those whom you gave me, because they
> are yours. All mine are yours, and yours are mine; and I have been

glorified in them. And now I am no longer in the world, but they are in the world, and I am coming to you. Holy Father, protect them in your name that you have given me, so that they may be one, as we are one. (John 17:9-11)

Long before the life of Jesus, the psalmist expressed a vision of God's persistent intention for humankind in this prayer:

May God be gracious to us and bless us and make his face to shine upon us, that your way may be known upon earth, your saving power among all nations. Let the peoples praise you, O God; let all the peoples praise you. Let the nations be glad and sing for joy, for you judge the peoples with equity and guide the nations upon earth. Let the peoples praise you, O God; let all the peoples praise you. The earth has yielded its increase; God, our God, has blessed us. May God continue to bless us; let all the ends of the earth revere him. (Ps. 67:1-7)

Such prayers inspire our prayers today.

My Lord and my God, I know not why you are so gracious to us, inviting us to participate in the communion of the Godhead, but you are that inclusive. As I share in this divine life, let it be the power that centers my life and the guide that inspires my prayers for others.

Silence

For God alone my soul waits in silence; from him comes my salvation. He alone is my rock and my salvation, my fortress; I shall never be shaken (Ps. 62:1-2).

Unquestionably the faithful have times when they experience divine silence. If the Spirit of God initiates all true prayer, what does God's silence mean?

All that I have said about prayer so far relates to words. When God appears to us in mystery, we offer praise. When God reveals steadfast love to us, we give thanks. When God's holiness breaks upon us, we confess. When God withdraws from us and does not deal with us according to our expectations, we complain. When God reveals an attentive generosity, we ask for the deepest desires of our hearts. When God comes to us as community, we participate in intercession for others. But what can be said about the silence of God?

I could say nothing and leave you with silence, but it seems unfair to raise so fundamental and important an issue and then walk away from it. As I said earlier, resist the easiest and most frequent explanation of God's silence. Don't let your first interpretive impulse accuse you of sin or spiritual failure; this makes God seem like an immature parent who becomes angry and stops speaking to a rule-breaking child. Such an interpretation of silence denies the goodness and generosity of God. The "silent treatment" also contradicts the Bible's most poignant response to a child's perversity — the waiting father whom we read about in the Parable of the Prodigal Son (Luke 15:11-24). The time has come to drop the "God is angry" explanation and look for a better answer.

Consider God's silence, if you require an explanation, as an invitation to listen. When God does not speak, it may mean that God is inviting you into the depths of your own life. With the absence of a bubbling assurance, God asks you to face your emptiness and listen to the longings and urgings that arise within you. In the silence you may also begin to hear the voices of your demons. It is best to face the negative force of a demon head-on. As popular Christian writer Parker Palmer suggests, "Climb on it and ride it into your depths."

The silence of God may also focus our hearts on their true needs. The noise of success added to come-and-go relationships with the Spirit keep the heart preoccupied so that it beats oblivious to the movement of God. When the silence comes, when this jolt from the Spirit unsettles us, God has our attention. God wants our attention to permit the longing for Godself within us to come to the fore. The longer and deeper the silence, the sharper the longing and the greater its persistence! When God ceases to speak in accustomed ways, we may need to hear him speak in a new dialect, like silence.

For those who have been praying a long time, speech sometimes obstructs communion with the divine. It's that way with lovers — after years of living with each other, they often don't need words. Sometimes the silence expresses more intimacy between two lovers than a thousand words could achieve. I think that God sometimes ceases to speak so that neither the divine word nor the human response will disrupt the depth of loving communion that takes place in the silence.

Although it may sound strange and contradictory, silence is part of the language that God speaks. The unspoken word that grasps us in the silence and the unuttered word of response make room for a union of the holy and the human. In this union God remains God, and I remain I, but we are touching in a deep and profound way. All that God wills to take place in me occurs, and all that God desires from me is given. And this miracle of transformation happens in the context of deep, mutual silence.

From another point of view, God's silence describes our encounter with the mystery. At first the appearance of the mystery prompts our praise of God, but after that initial response, the Spirit leads us to a place of wordlessness. The silence permits us to encounter the mystery, the inexpressible depth of the divine. For us there can be no comprehension, only awe-filled communion. No words grasp this communion; it is beyond language. In the silence the mystery makes itself present in wordless wonder.

Summary

In this chapter I have indicated two modes of primary GodSpeech — God's address to us and our address to God. My intention has been to call attention to how the essential nature of God inspires and shapes every form of prayer that arises in our hearts and flows from our lips. God's coming to us manifests God's initiative-taking nature. And our address to God is more than praising his greatness, pleading for our needs, or confessing our sins. It includes every form of prayer known to us. The Holy Spirit of God in us shapes our response according to the revelation of God's character and our situation.

The realization that God's Spirit inspires our prayer and that we are dealing with God deliver us from self-centered, self-seeking prayer. And it gives us great confidence to know that the Christ who prays in us offers the prayer God wishes to hear. And if God hears prayer, God will answer it.

QUESTIONS FOR REFLECTION AND DISCUSSION
1. What is the source of prayer?
2. How does the nature of God affect our prayer?
3. What is your interpretation of the silence of God?
4. How does seeing prayer as something inspired by God's nature affect the way you pray?

SUGGESTIONS FOR JOURNALING
1. Think about each aspect of God that inspires prayer and write the prayer that flows naturally from your heart.
2. Review your praying for the last few days. Write a reflection on how you see God's nature informing your prayer.

CHAPTER SEVEN

The Various Modes of GodSpeech

The voice of the LORD causes the oaks to whirl,
and strips the forest bare; and in his temple all say, "Glory!"
The LORD sits enthroned over the flood; the LORD sits
enthroned as king forever.

Psalm 29:9-10

Communication, as humans practice it, requires a mode — a tone of voice, a gesture, a look. Words certainly provide the building blocks of communication. Have you ever noticed how quickly the parents of newborns begin teaching them words? These words first name things and people, like "Mama" and "Dada," but quickly shift to directions — do this, don't do that. Gradually, young children acquire a collection of these sounds that connect names to things, people, and actions. By the time they enter the first grade, they have a vocabulary of about 6,000 words. These thousands of words include nouns to name, verbs to express action, and adjectives and adverbs to enrich and hold together the other parts.

But words are not their only means of communicating. Before children learn to speak, they learn the difference between a smile and a frown, a soft voice and a harsh one, and they know how to read situations before they can describe them. Their discernment of nonverbal cues precedes the acquisition of a vocabulary and develops more rapidly.

Just as children must acquire a vocabulary and the nonverbal signs that accompany it, we believers must learn the vocabulary of GodSpeech and the way of divine/human communication. God's speech to us comes in various ways that communicate meaning, direction, confirmation, and insight into the nature and intention of God. Like human language, the language of God has parts of speech that provide names and describe actions. And just as parents take the initiative in teaching children the various modes of human speech, God takes the initiative in teaching us the ways of GodSpeech, and over the span of a lifetime we develop an elementary comprehension of the language of God. Along the way, something like a basic speller or a grammar book would be helpful as we seek to acquire a beginner's knowledge of GodSpeech. Since we have neither, we must rely on the heavenly Parent. So how does God teach us divine speech?

There seems to be one major difference between the speech of God and parental speech — indirection. Earthly parents speak face to face, but our heavenly Parent, except on rare occasions, comes to us indirectly, through a medium. The various media range from ideas that appear in our minds, to events that occur in our lives, to our hearing through others the voice of God. Actually, everything that occurs in our lives has the potential of becoming GodSpeech, but for the most part, only those who expect and attend to GodSpeech hear it. Perhaps examining the various media will help us hear our divine Parent's disclosures.

GodSpeech through Creation

The language of creation has long mystified human beings. For ages our ancestors heard a voice in creation that spoke of the divine, but they did not know how to hear God in it. These ancient members of the race felt the awesomeness of the thunder and the lightning and fell on their faces in response, but without understanding the mystery. Still, they knew the mystery appeared to them in creation even when they could not name it.

In their groping for an understanding, they worshipped the sun and the moon and the stars. Since they were unable to distinguish the divine from the medium — trees, rocks, animals — almost everything became an object of reverence. This inability to separate the Creator from the creation led to totemism, animism, and idolatry. As simplistic as these responses may seem to us, they constitute humanity's first efforts to learn the vocabulary of GodSpeech, to hear the voice of God in the natural world and respond to it.

Later on, as the understanding of GodSpeech grew, the prayerful psalmist would write,

> The heavens are telling the glory of God; and the firmament proclaims his handiwork. Day to day pours forth speech, and night to night declares knowledge. There is no speech, nor are there words; their voice is not heard; yet their voice goes out through all the earth, and their words to the end of the world. In the heavens he has set a tent for the sun, which comes out like a bridegroom from his wedding canopy, and like a strong man runs its course with joy. Its rising is from the end of the heavens, and its circuit to the end of them; and nothing is hid from its heat. (Ps. 19:1-7)

This psalmist-poet no longer worshipped the creation but listened for the wordless voice to speak to him through the wonders of nature. Day and night it spoke without words, resounding throughout the world, expressing the divine.

In another place the psalmist says "deep calls to deep." The deep in the human heart cries out to the deep in creation; the voice of the Creator is heard, and the human heart gropes for a way to respond.

God has been speaking to humanity through the creation throughout the ages, from the psalmist's affirmation to Annie Dillard's recent book entitled *Teaching a Stone to Speak.* The first word of God, the primal word of God, was indeed the word spoken in creation.

GodSpeech through Ideas

God also teaches us the divine language through ideas that appear in our minds. These ideas both contain and mediate the language of God. Take Abraham, for example: God spoke to him and promised him a land and a people. This idea came into Abraham's mind with such clarity and conviction that he left all his security behind to obey God.

When the Bible states that God spoke to Abraham, I am convinced that the event was not unlike the way God speaks to us today. It is wise for us to put aside the notion of a voice shouting from the sky and place greater emphasis on hearing God in ideas that come to us. This will help us both to understand Abraham and to learn the grammar of GodSpeech.

Abraham faced all the questions that plague us. Like us, he wondered whether this promise came from God or was the product of his imagination. How could he be sure? He lacked many of the resources we have for discernment — the Scriptures, a believing community, and a long tradition. Furthermore, Abraham had to face the seeming self-centeredness of the promise: God would make him great, make his name great, and his offspring would bless the whole world. Quite a claim! Such apparent self-aggrandizement surely warrants suspicion.

What persuaded Abraham to believe that he heard God speak through the ideas that came rushing into his mind? For one thing, he did not expect to hear God make these audacious promises. So the unexpected nature of God's coming may have awakened him. For another thing, the force and clarity of the ideas no doubt strengthened his belief that the promises could be trusted. These ideas about a land and a people did not simply rustle through his mind like a spring breeze; they had the force and persistence of a March wind. The idea, unlike a casual visitor, settled into his awareness like a permanent guest, and there it confronted him day after day and in sleepless moments in the night. These experiences convinced him that the promise of a lineage and a land were not of his own making, that these notions were coming to him from beyond himself.

This event also prompted serious questions in Abraham's mind. No doubt he asked himself, "How can this be, since I am an old man? At her age, will my wife truly conceive and bear a son?" These questions suggest the seriousness with which Abraham took the ideas and the depth of their effect. But the strongest evidence that these ideas had a compelling effect on him lies in his courage to leave his home and kindred and follow the leading. When God rewarded his faith with an unexpected son," surely this sign deepened his assurance that God was speaking to him.

As you enroll in God's school of language, pay attention to the ideas that come to you. When even casual ideas come to your consciousness, pause and wonder where they came from. And notice especially those ideas that come unexpectedly and with great clarity. If they persist, give them extra attention. If the ideas are strong enough to evoke serious questions and inspire you to take new and risky directions in your life, then these ideas may well be GodSpeech.

I met a man in a large eastern city who had devoted his life to the poor. Mothers without husbands, sick children, and people evicted from their homes knocked on his door every day. He was ready with whatever help he could offer, and any help was welcomed.

I had to ask him the obvious questions: Why was he living in a poor, dangerous part of town with his wife and three daughters? Why was he risking his life in service to the poor? He explained that one day, while operating a family sporting-goods store in another city, an idea came to him. He began to think about serving the poor and forming small faith communities in people's homes. Although the idea was not fully fleshed out, it persisted, and he was so convicted of its rightness that he packed up his family and moved. Here is a modern Abraham who has begun to learn the language of God.

GodSpeech through People

Verification for the claim that God speaks through people is found in the prophets, wise men, and Christian witnesses, but the clearest example is Jesus himself. According to the Gospel of John, Jesus is the word of God made flesh (John 1:1-5, 14, 18). The manifestation of God in human flesh refers to the Incarnation and creates incarnational GodSpeech.

Numerous references in Scripture document that many individuals recognized the presence of God in Jesus. When Christ was brought to the temple as an infant, Simeon offered a prayer of thanksgiving to God: "My eyes have seen your salvation" (Luke 2:28). When Jesus was preaching and teaching, the demon-possessed man in the synagogue cried out, "I know who you are — the Holy One of God" (Luke 4:34). Andrew testified to his brother Peter, "We have found the Messiah" (John 1:41).

In his earthly life, Jesus communicated the presence of God through his person; and the record of his life and teaching still communicates a powerful sense of God. But the communication of the holy through the human did not cease with Jesus, or the apostles or the prophets. God still speaks through human beings; they are words in the vocabulary of God.

People who become words of God to others do not belong to a special category of saints, seers, or mystics. Often they are very ordinary people who think of themselves as simple believers. Also, strangely enough, God can and does speak through persons who do not claim to know God. Recognizing that God can speak through whomever God chooses, I have come to believe that God most often and most clearly speaks through authentic individuals — those who genuinely express in choices and actions who they really are. They do not try to impress others. In making this point I am in no way seeking to limit God. But there does seem to be something in the authentic individual that more easily permits the flow of the Spirit.

An old friend of mine, Paul Coulter, had the kind of integrity that seems to conduct GodSpeech. He was a simple man who helped others and found ways of expressing unselfish concern. I knew Paul well and had numerous talks with him, and the depth of his integrity was plainly evident in both word and deed. One day, in the midst of a conversation, he took a flat rock from his pocket and gave it to me. He said simply, "When I saw this rock at the lake yesterday, it made me think of you." I kept that rock for years. It was a constant reminder of Paul's act of remembrance and generosity. Each time I looked at it, I thought about the man through whom God spoke to me that fall morning.

As this example shows, God speaks through both the nature and the deeds of people. That Jesus was the Son of God expressed itself in his being as well as in his deeds — healing, feeding, and comforting. This mode of GodSpeech demands that we pay attention to what the people in our lives are doing. When, for example, we see them serving others, giving sacrificially on others' behalf, do we not often see Christ in their deeds?

One day I had registered at a small hotel in a mid-sized southern city. The minister who was picking me up was running a bit late. While I was waiting for him, I began a conversation with the desk clerk. She had punched in at 3:30 P.M. and would be there until eleven that night. As we spoke, she began to tell me a story of pain and sacrifice.

She must have been no older than nineteen or twenty. She held two full-time jobs — she was also a desk clerk and reservationist at another hotel. When I wondered at her industry, she told me that her mother was unable to work and had medical needs, so she worked two jobs seven days a week to provide for her care. This challenge had befallen her after her father's death; he had been killed just across the street from the college she had attended. His death had delayed her education and thrust her into a position of responsibility far too great for such a young woman. But she told her story without any apparent bitterness or resentment, and I heard God speak through her recounting of love and sacrifice.

I detected nothing that caused me to think that she was aware of being a word of God to me. And that is as it should be. If we try to be a word of God, we succeed only in calling attention to ourselves and not to God. Therefore, instruments of GodSpeech generally are unaware of God's voice speaking through them.

This story shows how word and deed are bound together. Indeed, God often speaks through human voices. Jesus' words, for example, expressed GodSpeech during his lifetime. God spoke through Jesus' words as well as his being and doing. After Jesus' death, God spoke through Jesus' followers. And God still speaks to us through other people, if we will only listen.

Some of us expect — or at least hope — to hear GodSpeech through a priest, pastor, prophet, or mystic. It is true that God does speak through chosen leaders. But I am suggesting that God speaks equally through friends, coworkers, neighbors — even strangers. This assertion may seem strange, but I believe it is true. God is always coming to us, always speaking to us, and we should pay attention to human words spoken to us because they may be words from God. Don't think of this experience of GodSpeech as weird or bizarre; it isn't. The Spirit of God speaks through ordinary human speech to confirm us or direct us or confront us.

For example, you might have a friend whose spouse is seriously ill. You visit the couple in the hospital, and as you prepare to leave, you say, "Everything will be all right." In a sense these words bring closure to the visit and offer encouragement. But if God chooses to use those words to speak to the uncertain couple, an assurance greater than your words will sustain them in their crisis.

GodSpeech through Visions

The mention of vision as a mode of GodSpeech frightens some people because it conjures up notions of hallucinations or mental illness. But according to the biblical record, God has spoken through visual images that appeared in people's minds. From a biblical point of view, we cannot overlook the significance of Peter's rooftop vision or of Cornelius's vision, which complements it. The Bible also speaks of the visions of Ezekiel and Isaiah and how deeply the two men were affected by them.

The vision mode of GodSpeech manifested itself in the church from its beginning. Polycarp, you will recall, had a vision of a burning pillow that convinced him he would die a fiery death. Another of the apostolic fathers, the Shepherd of Hermas, received numerous inspirations through visions. In the sixteenth century, Saint Teresa experienced visions, categorizing them as three types and testifying to their authenticity. In the first type of vision, a person has a heightened awareness of the presence of Christ in his or her life. In the second kind, a person begins to sense the living Christ with him or her through the use of images and meditation. In the third kind, a person receives an intellectual insight into a spiritual truth.[1]

Modern psychologists have noted that children often have an original vision for their lives. They express it as something they have always known they were meant to do or be. Both corporations and congregations speak of a vision for the body of persons they represent. And the word "vision" also points to a spiritual reality with great relevance for us today.

When we lift visions out of the realm of the bizarre and see them as images stamped in the mind, they lose some of their scariness. Most people have a vision for their lives; whether it is of God depends on the content and quality of the image. A vision of oneself winning the lottery and becoming a millionaire hardly qualifies as a God-given vision. On the other hand, a vision of living a sacrificial life through which one brings kindness into a pained world is quite clearly an authentic vision. To be without an authentic vision generally lands people in a world of meaninglessness where they have no sense of direction and end up in despair. Authentic vision is essential for the health of a person, a business, or a congregation. As a mode of GodSpeech, vision provides one significant way in which God influences the world.

I recall a young man who entered the seminary to prepare himself to serve. His vision was strong enough to draw him away from a good job and financial security. He exchanged these for the possibility of greater rewards than worldly success offered. Money and stature lost their appeal in the face of living another kind of life and the opportunity to make a difference in the world.

During the first years of his study, his vision lacked clarity, but his choices and direction seemed right. Then he joined a group on a mission trip to Jamaica, where he came face to face with poverty as he had never known it before. The needs of Third World people grasped and held his attention, and he found a place to serve in Mexico. He is still there, compelled by a vision.

---

1. Ben Campbell Johnson and Andrew Dreitcer, *Beyond the Ordinary: Spirituality for Church Leaders* (Grand Rapids: Eerdmans, 2001), pp. 73-74.

Sometimes a vision comes like a slow drip, finding its way into our consciousness drop by drop. At first we may not notice it, but drop by drop it clarifies itself by coloring our view of the future. Vision cannot be manufactured; it is always a gift that comes to us. Once in its grasp, we can reflect on it, enrich and broaden it, and permit it to shape our lives. In the end, a spiritual vision convicts us of its divine origin and gives us sufficient courage to follow its path, even at great risk.

A woman I met while teaching at Columbia Theological Seminary provides another interesting example of vision. She was a fine student with a trustworthy character, but her life was difficult. She had experienced a great deal of rejection in her life. As a young girl she had felt rejected by her parents when a third child had been born into the family. In her current situation she felt rejected by associates and also by friends.

One day she waited after class to tell me what had happened to her the night before. While she and her roommate were working on an assignment together, she had experienced a vision. This is how she described it:

> Last night my roommate read aloud the story of the Transfiguration and sought to visualize the event. As she did, images came to me: a picture of the mountain, the clouds, the thunder, and the voice. I felt like one of the disciples.
>
> Jesus said, "Come to me," and repeatedly I heard him saying, "Listen." Then he said, "I love you; I love you." I was overcome with emotion. I began to cry.
>
> Then I had a vision of Jesus. He looked like the picture I had seen in Sunday school literature. He took me down a long path until we came to a small castle, my hiding place. He gave me a candle, opened the door, and together we went in. There was a fire in the fireplace. He washed my feet and gave me a pair of slippers. Then he said, "Susan, you wash the feet of the others."

Through this vision this woman's wounds were healed, and she discovered a new direction for her life.

Godspeech through God's Own Voice

The Bible reports stories in which it appears that God spoke in an audible voice. In discussing Abraham, I have emphasized that he probably had an idea appear in his mind and that God probably spoke in his mind rather than in an audible voice — though no one knows for sure. Luke, who wrote the book of Acts, declares that Saint Paul heard Jesus speak to him in an audible voice. In one account, those who traveled with Paul heard the voice (Acts 9:7). When John, the writer of the Fourth Gospel and the book of Revelation, was in exile on the Isle of Patmos, he heard Jesus speaking: "I was in the spirit on the Lord's Day, and I heard behind me a loud voice like a trumpet . . ." (Rev. 1:10).

A close examination of the records of the church through the centuries yields numerous reports of audible messages from God. What are we to make of these? And how does God speak to us today?

I have never experienced an audible word from God, but I have spoken with one person who testifies to having had this experience. A student of mine who was of Jewish descent felt profound confusion about Jesus when he was confronted with the gospel story. In desperation he cried out to God, "Is Jesus the Messiah?" According to his testimony, the voice answered audibly: "He is the Messiah."

Leanne Payne, a Christian author and counselor, also writes about hearing the voice of God. It happened to her only once, but she remembers the experience very vividly. She was awakened from a very deep sleep. She saw nothing, but she knew that she was awake and not dreaming. The Lord spoke six words, and they were the words of Saint Paul: "To me, to live is Christ." These words came at a time of crisis in her life and gave her the courage to confront her doubts and fears.[2]

In both these modern situations, the question remains: Did God speak to these individuals audibly, so that others present could have heard the words, or did God cause these words to appear powerfully in their minds? I believe it is more likely that these were miracles of hearing rather than audible speech from God.

---

2. Payne, *Listening Prayer* (Grand Rapids: Baker Books, 1994), p. 179.

GodSpeech through Our Imagination

I think there are many ways in which our imagination becomes an instrument of GodSpeech, but most often I experience God speaking to me through my writing. Sometimes writing in my journal provides the context for God to speak; at other times, the speech comes when I am developing a class or writing a book.

In one particular instance, God's speaking through my imagination happened like this. I began thinking about another class to teach. The topic of "the spirituality of the church" came into my mind. As I began to think about the content of the course, I pulled out an envelope and jotted down a few ideas about the spirituality of the pastor and the spiritually of the people. Then I began to elaborate on these ideas. Soon I saw that I was dreaming not only of a course but perhaps also of a book.

I then copied the fifteen or twenty ideas from the envelope into a notebook. As I worked with these ideas, I experienced the creative power of imagination and the energy to keep writing, and the ideas began to grow. And as is so often the case, new ideas began to pour out of my mind, and I created as I wrote. I had thoughts that I had never had before, and the logic, energy, and power of the ideas began to erupt like a small volcano. Soon I had forty or fifty pages of notes on the ideas that were bubbling in my mind.

When I am in this "zone," I am very excited about the ideas; I wake up every morning with a desire to get up and write. I feel the rush of ideas cascading into my mind.

I cannot explain how this unfolding comes. In this particular case, the process began with an invitation to teach a summer class, then accelerated with a few ideas about the topic and the organization and expansion of them. Certain parts of the process remain a mystery to me. I cannot explain why I got some ideas and not others. Once these major ideas were in place, I began to break them down into logical parts, which would help others see what I was thinking and feeling about these matters. When I began writing, these ideas took on a life of their own and grew. They seemed to direct the way that the writing went.

When I write, I am always amazed at what comes out. I find myself writing about things I did not know I knew; thoughts come that are as instructive to me as they are to the reader. Writing provides a context for my imagination to hear the voice inside me. I discover information that I did not know I possessed, I encounter new images, and I experience a compelling fascination with what occurs. Where do these ideas come from? Perhaps from God.

GodSpeech through Events

Once a group of hunters debated about the finest music in the world. "The cuckoo calling from the tree," said one.

"The greatest of all music," said another, "is the ring of a spear on a shield."

"Yes, yes!" the group echoed.

But others named the bellowing of a stag across water, the baying of hounds in the distance, the song of a lark, the laughter of a child, and the whisper of a person in awe.

"All these sounds are good," said the captain of the hunt.

"What do you think is the greatest?" the group asked the captain.

"The music of what happens — that is the finest music in the world." The music of what happens. What a wonderful observation!

And we must listen to the music of what is happening because it is not only the finest in the world; it is also one of God's primary ways of speaking to us. According to well-known priest and theologian James Fenhagen, "Every event, every encounter carries within it the potential for an encounter with God. And as these events pass and are carried in memory, the potential for dialogue remains."[3] And the great philosopher and writer Martin Buber once wrote that it is "in the signs of life which happen to us that we are addressed."[4]

---

3. Fenhagen, *More than Wanderers: Spiritual Discipline for Christian Ministry* (New York: Seabury Press, 1981), p. 35.

4. Buber, *Between Man and Man* (New York: Macmillan, 1965), p. 14.

Much of our lives are filled with ordinary events that seem to bear no message from God. On an average day, we rise from sleep, take a shower, have coffee, and then dash to work. During the day we answer phone calls, send e-mails, attend meetings, and ply our trade. From our first waking moment in the morning until we lie down to rest at night, our lives are filled with events. Most days bring nothing big, bold, or life-changing — and yet they can still be filled with significance. This is one area that modern literature has done justice to — even if it does not give credit to the Giver. In *Care of the Soul,* for example, Thomas Moore urges us to recognize the sacred in the ordinary events of our lives.

If we stopped to reflect, would our days seem so ordinary?

Even the most apparently ordinary of days can be marked by a special meeting or an unexpected occurrence. Most of us can look back on a number of days that were marked by a chance meeting, a phone call, an accident of circumstance, a penetrating insight, a conversation, or another of a myriad of seemingly small events that today hold special significance for us. And as we recall those events, we recognize that our lives are different because of them. When we recognize the influence of these occurrences, it makes us wonder if under the veil of the ordinary God isn't whispering a word in our ears. I think this is what James Fenhagen is suggesting when he says, "Reflection on life experience becomes itself an act of prayer because it seeks to take seriously the address of God."[5]

During some of these "ordinary" days, events coalesce with a kind of energy that immediately gets our interest and attention. These days have a kinship to the day that a burning bush attracted Moses' attention and stopped him long enough so that he heard God's voice. I myself have had some ordinary days in which a "God-event" happened. When I was in school, a fellow student asked me an all-important question: If Jesus should come today, would I be on his side? Years later, a friend happened to tell me that his school was searching for a professor of evangelism — and I became that professor. More years later, my colleagues in the pastoral area at Columbia Theological Seminary affirmed me in my

5. Fenhagen, *More than Wanderers,* p. 36.

proposal to teach courses on Christian spirituality. In each of these experiences, several events came together so that I heard a confirmation, a direction, or an assurance from God. In my case, being immediately aware of God's voice seems to happen less often than becoming aware of God's address through a reflection on past events. Occasionally, however, I am aware of GodSpeech in the moment that it occurs.

Whether we hear the voice in the moment or when we look back at certain events, God does seem to speak in clusters of events. Take Peter's becoming a disciple of Jesus, for example. He heard about Jesus from his brother Andrew: the first event. After that he no doubt went to listen to Jesus and visited Jesus' home: a second event. Later on, Jesus came by Peter's "workplace," where he was washing and mending his fishing nets, and borrowed his boat: a third event. While Jesus spoke, Peter was listening to his message, and when Jesus finished speaking, he directed Peter's next fishing venture: a fourth event. Fish filled the nets and then two boats to overflowing: a fifth event. At this point Peter's mind was opened to wonder: a sixth event. He fell at Jesus' knees and heard the invitation "Come, follow me": the seventh event. Each of these smaller events combined to form the large event labeled "the call of Peter." Peter's call grew out of the confluence of these smaller happenings and became clear when Jesus invited him to be a disciple.

The illustrations that I have cited tend to be life-changing directions from God, yet most of them have come through the ordinary events of a day, through small, seemingly insignificant encounters and occurrences. Disciples intent upon listening for God in the happenings of their lives have found it productive to list the events of a typical day and reflect on them as a way of hearing God. And they often do! The presence of the Spirit inspires the human imagination to see in the events of a day the initiative of God.[6]

---

6. Ben Campbell Johnson, *Living before God: Deepening Our Sense of the Divine Presence* (Grand Rapids: Eerdmans, 2000), pp. 69-83.

Practical Applications

GodSpeech through Dreams

From the distant past until today, dreams have always fascinated people. Dreams have made predictions, conferred divine assurance, warned of coming danger, and given direction to God's people, among a host of other things. I think we too easily write off dreams as irrelevant to our lives today, and this may be a mistake. Certainly Jung and Freud and other psychologists have placed great emphasis on dreams, and spiritual leaders like Morton Kelsey have focused on dreams as a way of God's speaking to people.

The birth and early life of Jesus is surrounded with dream activity. Joseph has a dream in which he is told that he should take Mary for his wife (Matt. 1:20); the Wise Men are warned in a dream not to return to Herod (Matt. 2:12); a dream directs Joseph to take Jesus and his wife to Egypt (Matt. 2:13); a dream next directs Joseph to return home (Matt. 2:19-20); and in yet another dream Joseph is warned not to stop in Judea but to return to Galilee (Matt. 2:22). At the end of Jesus' life, when he is on trial, Pilate's wife sends a message to her husband that he should have nothing to do with Jesus because she had a dream about him. Perhaps dreams are sometimes more than our unconscious mind working out conflicts or venting emotions. Maybe God still speaks through dreams.

I recently attended a planning meeting in which the leader was getting to know us according to our practices, among other things. He asked how many of us kept a record of our dreams. All the participants moved to the left side of the room except one. One person stood alone on the right side of the room because he was the only one who kept a log of his dreams. Perhaps this indicates the lack of seriousness with which many of us take our dreams.

Some time ago I was conducting a retreat. During the course of it, one participant asked me why I was interested in spirituality. I told him that I thought the roots of my interest grew out of my childhood fear of death, but there were also other contributors to my passion. Later that day the same man pulled me aside and said, "I am seventy-seven years old, and I have suddenly realized that I am going to die. I've always known it, but now I feel it. And it has troubled me."

He continued, "But I had a dream that spoke to me. In the dream I saw clearly that the God who made this world and planned all the wonderful things in it has more in store for us in heaven than we have ever been able to comprehend." The man was at peace. Perhaps God did speak to him through the dream.

In a doctoral class that I taught once, a woman minister spoke about her resistance to speaking to a dying woman about Christ. In seminary she had been taught that a minister should never bring up the subject of Christ to another person, but should wait for him or her to ask. Despite her reluctance, she did visit the woman and talked with her about the Savior and about facing death. Then the two prayed together.

After speaking with the woman, the minister explained, she felt guilty. She had violated the guidance of her pastoral care instructor, so she felt conflicted about what she had done.

As she continued telling her story, she said, "That night I had a dream in which God came to me and said, 'You were right. What you did was good.'" The next day the dying woman's family called to thank her. As it turned out, she had met with the woman about fifteen minutes before she died.

The minister explained that she felt liberated and affirmed because in a dream the Lord told her that she had done the right thing. Should she believe that God spoke to her?

Sometimes I have dreams and wonder what they mean. I recall dreaming about preaching to a small group of fifty or sixty people gathered in a small room. I was preaching on the subject of sin, and suddenly I found myself struggling to recall the three major points I wished to make.

While I was groping for the ideas, a woman spoke up. "I don't feel like I need what you are saying."

I said to her, "I'm not too interested in it myself; this is not what I need, either."

"What do you need?" someone asked the woman.

"I don't know," she replied.

At that point we moved into a new room, and I overheard someone say, "I've never seen a preacher respond to a person like that."

What did this dream mean? What does it say about me? Does it suggest that I am a preacher in need of affirmation? Is the Lord conveying to me that I take people's responses to my message seriously? This dream stayed with me because it contained an element of truth that spoke to me. I believe there was and is a message in it for me.

GodSpeech through Scripture

The Bible is the story of God. It is a people's experience of the mystery told and retold in narrative form, inspired by the Spirit, preserved in a tradition, and made available to us in a text that still speaks today. To hear the Word of God is to hear God himself. So read it, listen to it, reflect upon it, contemplate it, and absorb it into your soul.

In the Hebrew-Christian tradition, serious devotees have always turned to the normative word in Scripture to listen for the voice of God. From the beginning, the makers of the tradition believed that God had spoken to them. These central figures like Abraham, Moses, David, and the prophets narrated their experiences with the God who spoke. As the stories were told and retold, the community listened for God to speak repeatedly through those stories. After years of living by an oral tradition, they recorded the extended story and preserved it as sacred scripture. Because the people so frequently heard God speak again through the Torah, the Writings, the Psalms, and the prophets, we call the book the Word of God.

A similar development occurred after Jesus' life and ministry on earth. His disciples recalled his deeds and his words and retold them, and their listeners heard Christ speak through the disciples' narratives. Two criteria for selecting each book in the New Testament were the authenticity of its message and its power to communicate the voice of Christ to its listeners.

In the Christian tradition, reading Scripture texts and listening to their exposition has provided the norm for all GodSpeech. But neither reading the texts nor listening to them preached guarantees that you will hear God speak. These two acts can give you information about what God has said, but to hear God yourself requires more. For you to truly hear God, the words in the Bible must be enlivened, particularized, personalized, and made contemporary in a dynamic way. This amazing transformation not only can but does occur regularly.

How does Scripture come alive in this way? The words on the pages of the Bible are like a corpse in a tomb until they receive life through the Spirit. When the Spirit enters into a text, it rises from death, commands your attention, enlightens you, and draws you into its truth. This movement of the Spirit in the text transforms it from human speech into GodSpeech.

Through the Spirit, a message for another time and place and people becomes a personal word in the concrete situation of your life. In a powerful way, words written for others connect with your life experience, thus making the ancient text contemporary and personalized.

But the Spirit not only causes the text to connect with your situation; it also makes it speak truth to you. As you read, it seems that the truth of this biblical text knows you, knows you even better than you know yourself. How often have you begun to read a text only to discover that soon the text is reading you! You have the sense that the Voice in the text, or beyond the text, is speaking to you personally.

Perhaps Sam's story will clarify what I am describing. Sam had been estranged from God for a number of years. But several years ago, when faced with a job crisis, he began attending a community church in his hometown, and there he learned the meaning of God's love for him. Not only did he learn of this love; he also experienced it in the fellowship of the congregation. As he engaged in ancient Christian practices like prayer, Scripture reading, and regular worship, he changed for the better, and his family benefitted from these changes. He was kinder and more considerate of them, and he became more generous in his giving and more charitable in his judgment.

Before his renewal, Sam had been unfaithful to his wife on more than one occasion. All this changed when he came back to God. However, after several years of faithful living, Sam was on a business trip for his company and awakened to find a strange woman in his bed. This failure bothered him greatly; he was overwhelmed by guilt. He tried to rationalize his mistake as a meaningless act, but he could not shed his sense of failure, and he turned against himself. Depression set in. When his wife and Christian friends inquired what was wrong, he could not admit the truth.

After his mistake, Sam neglected his diligent reading of the Bible. But one day he decided to turn to the Scriptures for help. While thumbing through the Bible, his eye fell on Psalm 32, and he read these verses:

> While I kept silence, my body wasted away through my groaning all day long. For day and night your hand was heavy upon me; my strength was dried up as by the heat of summer. Then I acknowledged my sin to you, and I did not hide my iniquity; I said, "I will confess my transgressions to the LORD," and you forgave the guilt of my sin. Therefore let all who are faithful offer prayer to you; at a time of distress, the rush of mighty waters shall not reach them. You are a hiding place for me; you preserve me from trouble; you surround me with glad cries of deliverance.
>
> I will instruct you and teach you the way you should go; I will counsel you with my eye upon you. Do not be like a horse or a mule, without understanding, whose temper must be curbed with bit and bridle, else it will not stay near you. (Ps. 32:3-9)

This text, written over three thousand years ago, preserved and edited by devout men, spoke to Sam's need today. As Sam read the words about keeping silent and suffering dryness of soul, suddenly this text was not for someone three millennia ago but for him, for Sam, who was keeping silent about his sin.

Through the text he saw the solution to his problem: to confess his sin to God, because God forgave the offender's sin. He was gripped by the psalmist's conviction that he too could be forgiven, and forgiven in an instant.

The perspective of the text shifted when he read, "I will instruct you and teach you the way that you should go; I will counsel you with my eye upon you." These words assured him that God was watching over him and directing him even during this dark and challenging period of his life.

Further counsel came in the subsequent verse: "Do not be like a horse or a mule, without understanding, whose temper must be curbed with bit and bridle." Without the bit and bridle, the horse or mule will wander away. Don't wander away from God. Don't be someone who resists God's rule. Obey God and God's precepts.

Through this text written years ago, the Spirit spoke to Sam in a marvelous way that commanded his attention and called forth a confession. Afterward he felt forgiven and restored in his fellowship with God.

GodSpeech through Silence

What more can I say about silence? In the preceding chapter we have discussed in detail how God can speak to us in silence. But perhaps this additional thought will be fruitful. If we turn to the study of linguistics, we discover that an important element of human speech is the use of silence, where and how long a pause occurs. The length of a pause affects a syllable, a word, a phrase, a clause, a complete sentence, an entire conversation.

Where and how long we are silent is critical in human speech. Why not in GodSpeech as well? Is there not communication in the divine pauses?

In all these diverse ways God still speaks to humankind. Our task is to learn to listen for God and to respond to what God says.

QUESTIONS FOR REFLECTION AND DISCUSSION
1. How would you prioritize these modes of God's speech to us, from the most to the least dependable?
2. Which of these forms of God's communication to us do you find in the brief biographies in Chapters Four and Five?
3. Review your own life thoughtfully. Which of these modes of GodSpeech have you experienced?
4. How could your congregation better help people to recognize God's intervention in their lives?

Practical Applications

There are a number of exercises that will help you recognize each of the modes of GodSpeech. I offer you two examples.

1. Get seated comfortably. Take three or four minutes to breathe deeply several times and feel your body become completely relaxed. Slowly pick up your journal or turn to your computer and begin to write the ideas that come to your mind. Don't force them — let them flow into your consciousness as they will. When no ideas come to you, abide in the deep silence. When you finish this exercise, read over the ideas you have recorded and wonder what God might be saying to you through them.

2. Choose an ordinary day and list the movements of the day — that is, the little shifts in activity, thought, and relationship. Then look at this bare-bones structure of the day and re-imagine it. Wonder where God was at work in your day. Begin to write what comes to you as you keep asking about each event and God's possible place in it.

CHAPTER EIGHT

Understanding the Syntax
of GodSpeech

May the LORD give strength to his people! May the LORD bless his people with peace!

Psalm 29:11

God is always coming to us and as presence is always speaking to us. Having reviewed the history of the various ways that God engages in divine discourse, the practical and persistent inquirer asks how GodSpeech occurs in our lives today and how these various modes of GodSpeech relate to each other. Rather than being isolated words or actions of God, GodSpeech most often combines different modes to communicate the presence and purpose of God. These various modes God employs (which we explored in the preceding chapter) are, metaphorically speaking, the syntax of GodSpeech.

Syntax derives from two Greek words that mean "with" and "order." Thus syntax, as we use the term grammatically, refers to the orderly arrangement of words and phrases so that they effectively communicate meaning. When we seek ways to interpret the message or messages being sent from God, we need an understanding of the relationship of God's various modes of speech — an understanding of the syntax of GodSpeech.

For example, God may have promised Abraham land and offspring, and this communication may have been God actually speaking to Abraham or vivid ideas coming into his mind. But there was a larger context in which this communication came to Abraham. Recall that he was a man of wealth but dissatisfied with his state of soul. Is there not GodSpeech in his dissatisfaction? He tells his father and family about God's promises, and they confirm his revelation by sending family members with him on the journey. Is this not God speaking through his family's response? And when the promise of a son materializes in Isaac, does this event not constitute GodSpeech as well? So when I suggest that each aspect of this event is a communication of God, I mean that these unfolding events order, clarify, and define God's intention for Abraham. Or we could say that the ordering of these supporting events forms the syntax of GodSpeech.

Most often one of these modes of GodSpeech will be central in revealing God's person and God's intention, but the principal mode is also surrounded with other "parts of speech" that help us understand God's discourse.

The speech of God usually consists of more than one word; it often comes in a constellation. If we take a close look at GodSpeech in the life of Augustine, who is central to the development of the Christian faith, we will see with depth and clarity the meaning of the syntax of GodSpeech.

Augustine of Hippo

From the beginning, Augustine seemed destined to be a central figure in developing the thought of the Christian church. He was born in 354 in the town of Tagaste, Italy, where today there stands an Arab village near the eastern border of Algeria. His father was a pagan, but his mother, Monica, was a faithful Christian.

In his early years Augustine lived a kind of divided life. On the one hand, he was a worldly man who was obsessed with sex and enslaved by his passions. On the other hand, he studied widely and sought answers to his deep questions about the meaning of his life. He experiemented with a variety of philosophies and religions. The Manichaeans offered him a philosophy that did not condemn his profligate ways, and for several years he followed their teachings. During this time he kept a concubine and fathered a son about whom we know very little. But in the end Manichaeism proved inadequate to answer his questions and still the restlessness of his soul.

The turning point in his life, and the incident that we want to explore in some depth, occurred when he was thirty-three years old. He had immersed himself in pagan philosophy, read some Christian writings, listened to the preaching of Ambrose, bishop of Milan — and still he found no peace. I have no doubt that God was speaking to him through all his searching and thinking and yearning during this time, but the fulfillment of his longing did not come.

In his *Confessions,* Augustine gives us a full account of that final period of searching and aching and finally hearing God speak to him. It is clear from this recounting that he experienced various modes of GodSpeech coming together to communicate God's word to him. Exploring his penetrating analysis of his encounter with God offers us a grand model for illustrating the syntax of GodSpeech.

Ponticianus, a fellow countryman from North Africa who was employed by the Roman state, came to visit with Augustine. Apparently the visit had not been planned, because Ponticianus showed up unannounced at the villa in Milan where Augustine and his mother were staying. The two men had been conversing for just a few minutes when Ponticianus noticed a book lying on a nearby game table. He picked it up and was surprised to find that it was a copy of the letters of Saint Paul. Since Augustine was a teacher of rhetoric, he probably had assumed that the book would be on that subject, so when he saw that it contained Paul's letters, he smiled. He then confessed to Augustine that he was a Christian and was very pleased to know that Augustine was acquainting himself with Scripture.

As the conversation continued, Ponticianus recalled the story of Saint Anthony, describing how he had forsaken a fortune to make his way into the desert in search of a relationship with God. Augustine had

never heard of Anthony, his quest for God, or his role in the early begin-
nings of monastic communities. The discussion of monasteries reminded Ponticianus of an experience long past, when he had accompanied the Roman emperor to Trier, an outpost of Roman authority on the
Mosel River in Germany. While the emperor attended the gladiatorial
games, Ponticianus and three of his associates were strolling in the gardens near the city walls. Walking two by two, they soon separated, with
Ponticianus and his colleague leaving the other two men, who wandered
off to a nearby cottage. There they found a book about Anthony written
by Athanasius. When they began reading it, they felt powerfully drawn
to the monastic life, and then and there made their commitment to it.
About the time these two men made their decision, Ponticianus discovered them and indicated that it was time to leave because the day was
drawing to a close and the games had ended. But the two men told him
and his companion about their decision and begged them not to stand in
their way.

While recounting this story of God's call, Ponticianus did not realize what a stirring impact his narration was having on Augustine. For
months he had been struggling with making the life-changing decision
to follow Christ, without success — and the decision had seemed so
quick and easy for Ponticianus's companions. But, unlike these two
men, Augustine had been praying, "Give me chastity and continence,
but not yet."[1] In this desperate prayer Augustine was asking for the restraint of the desires that controlled his life — but not too soon. Now
Augustine felt that Ponticianus was looking into his very soul and
speaking directly to his struggle. His words had an unsettling power
that gnawed at Augustine and overwhelmed him with shame.

Ponticianus left when the conversation was finished, but the torment did not depart from Augustine's soul. He was a prisoner to his
passions, which bound him like chains so that he felt helpless to move in
this new direction. In a dramatic figure of speech, he states that God set
him behind himself, and then turned him around to look at himself.

---

1. *The Confessions of St. Augustine,* translated by John K. Ryan (Garden City, N.Y.:
Image Books, 1960), p. 194.

When he saw a corrupted image of his personhood, he realized how separated he was from God.

But God did not leave him alone in his distress. Recalling his struggle, Augustine says, "Within the hidden depths of my soul, O Lord, you urged me on."[2] Was not this urging the voice of God speaking in the depths of Augustine's being, a presence and a communication so near and powerful that he was not left to his own devices?

Augustine's longing intensified, and his eagerness for God began to possess him. "Let it be done now," he prayed. "Now let it be done."[3]

Such a strong longing for God never goes unchallenged. At the same time that Augustine prayed for deliverance, he heard the voices of his passions inside his head asking, "Do you cast us off?" He feared that if he turned away from these passions, the decision would be permanent, and the thought both terrified and paralyzed him. Whether this was the voice of habit or passion or the devil, we do not know for sure; we do know that Augustine's turning away from his old life was not easy. The struggle was intense. But in the midst of the struggle he had a vision of "continence" speaking with him.

As Augustine explains it, "There appeared to me the chaste dignity of continence, serene and joyous, but in no wanton fashion, virtuously alluring, so that I would come to her and hesitate no longer."[4] The voice that spoke to him sounds very much like the voice of Christ. His description reminds us of Rudolf Otto's experience of the Holy, which he described with the phrase *mysterium et fascinans.* He was fascinated at the thought of being in relationship with God, and the desire drew him irresistibly to the Holy One. This, I believe, is the seduction of God, which fits with this "chaste dignity of continence" speaking to the struggling Augustine.

Augustine continues his description of his encounter with "continence": "She smiled upon me with an enheartening mockery, as if to say: 'Cannot you do what these youths and these maidens do? . . . The

---

2. *The Confessions of St. Augustine,* pp. 199-200.
3. *The Confessions of St. Augustine,* p. 200.
4. *The Confessions of St. Augustine,* p. 201.

Lord their God gave me to them. Why do you stand on yourself, and thus stand not at all? Cast yourself on him. Have no fear. He will not draw back and let you fall. Cast yourself trustfully on him: he will receive you and he will heal you.'"[5]

The struggle that had been intensified by his conversation with Ponticianus and clarified by his vision of continence so shook Augustine that he was on the verge of tears, and at the time his friend Alypius was with him. Feeling embarrassed by his distress, he asked Alypius to remain in the house while he went into the garden to be alone. There Augustine fell on his knees under a fig tree and began to weep. As he wept, a plaintive cry crossed his lips: "How long, how long? Tomorrow and tomorrow? Why not now? Why not in this very hour an end to my uncleanness?"[6]

While still weeping and praying, he heard the voice of a child in the neighboring house chanting, "Take up and read. Take up and read." He was so startled that he stopped weeping long enough to wonder whether there was a child's game that involved this singsong refrain. He could think of none. It then occurred to him that the words were directed to him: this was a command of God to him! So he took the child's words as a direction to open the book of Paul's letters and read the first passage he came upon. After all, Ponticianus had told him how Anthony had been directed by words from the Gospel.

Augustine describes what he did next: "So I hurried back to the spot where Alypius was sitting, for I had put there the volume of the apostle when I got up and left him. I snatched it up, opened it, and read in silence the chapter on which my eyes fell: 'Not in rioting and drunkenness, not in chambering and impurities, not in strife and envying; but put you on the Lord Jesus Christ, and make no provision for the flesh in its concupiscences'" (Rom. 13:13-14). When he finished reading this passage, he recalls, "Instantly, . . . as if before a peaceful light streaming into my heart, all the dark shadows of doubt fled away."[7]

The Word of God came to him with such gentleness and power that

---

5. *The Confessions of St. Augustine*, p. 201.

6. *The Confessions of St. Augustine*, p. 202.

7. *The Confessions of St. Augustine*, p. 202.

it wiped away the struggle and pain he had been experiencing. At this point the burden was no longer on Augustine — what decisions he could make or what habits he could overcome — because the grace of God had come to him and changed him.

When peace came to his divided and angst-ridden soul, he turned to Alypius and told him everything that had happened. When Alypius heard his testimony, he took the letters of Paul and read the very next verse in Romans: "Now him that is weak in the faith, take unto you" (Rom. 14:1). He applied these words to himself and made the decision to join Augustine in his new life.

The story of Augustine is not complete without the next scene in the drama. Both Alypius and Augustine sought out Augustine's mother to tell her what had happened. When she heard the good news, she rejoiced and blessed God's name. From the day Augustine was born, she had prayed that he might know the love of God and the joyous communion of the church. Now her prayers had been answered.

The Syntax of GodSpeech in Augustine's Story

If there are patterns in God's way of self-disclosure — that is, symbolically speaking, the syntax of GodSpeech — Augustine provides a good model to illustrate the sequence of revelatory events. In what follows, I will analyze Augustine's experience, identify the parts of GodSpeech that mark it, and describe their organization and relationship. With this exercise I hope to concretely illustrate the syntax of GodSpeech and what we may learn about the formation of GodSpeech. This spiritual endeavor compares to diagramming a sentence because it demands that we name the parts of speech and show their relationship to each other.

Two cautions must be kept in mind as we pursue this enterprise: first, when I speak of the syntax of GodSpeech, I am using the word "syntax" metaphorically; and second, I am fully aware that the rules of divine speech cannot be rigid and exacting but only suggestive. That said, I am confident that the story of Augustine will be instructive for us.

What are the modes of speech that we encounter in Augustine's life, and how do they relate to his transformation and contribute to his be-coming one of the most significant thinkers and leaders in the Christian church?

Searching

What becomes obvious to us from the outset is Augustine's searching spirit. A yearning for purpose and fulfillment drives both his intellec-tual and his fleshly quest. He becomes well-educated and well-read and explores various philosophies and religions. He also lives for the pas-sions of the flesh. But neither effort produces the reward he seeks.

Some would say that this searching spirit characterizes every young person in search of their identity and destiny. Perhaps it is the human predicament. But Augustine's search is one of desperation; it is more than a typical search for identity and meaning. His urgency seems to be driven by a power and a spirit beyond himself.

I think that the urgency of his quest is the work of God. I think it is God who is speaking to Augustine, creating in his heart the yearning for purpose and fulfillment. For most of his thirty-three years, Augustine had probably thought that his restlessness sprang only from himself, but after that moment of encounter in Milan, he knew that God had been at work in him for a long time.

Later he wrote these now-famous words: "Thou has made us for thyself, O God, and our hearts are restless until they rest in Thee." This statement suggests that upon reflection Augustine saw God in his searching; the Spirit was drawing him to Godself.

The hunger and urgency of his searching indicate the prior initiative of God in awakening and drawing Augustine to him.

Providential Occurrences

Augustine's searching is impacted by the unscheduled visit of Ponti-cianus. At a time in Augustine's life when his inner hunger has turned to pain and conflict, a fellow countryman and friend comes for an unannounced visit. During the visit he rejoices in Augustine's reading of Paul's letters, acknowledges that he is a Christian, tells Augustine the story of Saint Anthony, and relates a story about two friends who read about Saint Anthony's life and decided to become monks.

The visit itself seems to be a part of GodSpeech. Ponticianus, a man who works intimately with the emperor and is held in high esteem by other officials, makes an unplanned visit, then confesses to Augustine that he is a believer. Could it be that God had a hand in his decision to visit Augustine? Doesn't it seem somewhat strange that he appeared at the very moment that the war in Augustine's breast was raging at its fiercest?

The content of Ponticianus's conversation also becomes a medium of GodSpeech to Augustine. First Ponticianus speaks about Saint Anthony and his hearing Christ's call through the word of Scripture. Augustine is amazed by the purity of Anthony's devotion, and also struck by how Anthony's life overlapped his own: Anthony died in 356, two years after Augustine's birth. Next Ponticianus relates how two companions came to Christ by reading Anthony's story, which gives Augustine a vision of his struggle and one way of resolution.

I see the providence of God in the visit of Ponticianus at this particular time; the content of his conversation also manifests the providence of God. Indeed, God spoke through Ponticianus.

The Inner Voice

The inner voice in Augustine's soul is the voice of God speaking to him. Augustine tells us of his conversation with the Lord in quite explicit terms: "Within the hidden depths of my soul, O Lord, you urged me on." He does not tell us in detail how this voice urged him on, but he suggests that God spoke and that he received courage to continue in his quest. Maybe it was a quiet assurance of the divine presence. Or it could have been the confidence that he had chosen the right road. Then again, it could have been words or ideas appearing in his mind, reassuring him that his struggle was meaningful and that he would come through it. Whatever this voice said, in whatever way it manifested itself, Augustine drew strength from its urging.

Prayer

By prayer I mean the primary GodSpeech that responds to the divine initiative. We have defined primary human speech as the speech we employ to address God directly. If God was indeed addressing Augustine through his restlessness, through Ponticianus, and through his inner voice, Augustine was responding directly to God when he prayed. His prayers sound like one side of an urgent conversation.

In a sense, the whole of the *Confessions* is an extended address to God, an elongated prayer. Augustine is praying his life before God. Often he directly addresses God, as he did when he prayed, "Give me chastity and continence, but not yet." Later he prayed without any ambivalence: "Let it be done now. Now let it be done." These two instances illustrate Augustine's openness in the presence of God.

The Voice of Evil

In this narrative we encounter not only God speaking to Augustine but also the devil speaking to him. If we are too sophisticated to speak of evil in a personalized form, then we can call this a dialogue between Augustine and his raging passions, or his self-will, or the spirit of evil. Whatever the name given this negative force that Augustine struggled with, we all know about it. It is within us too. When we would do good, evil is present to hinder us. When God calls us, the perverse spirit suggests excuses. When our minds are set upon God and God's will for us, the detractor turns our heads toward self-will and disobedience. Call it what you will — we all encounter the voice of a power that draws us away from the highest and the best.

Augustine heard the voices of his temptations asking him, "Do you cast us off?" This startling question terrified him as he considered giving up his sinful habits forever. He knew that turning toward God meant that he had to permanently renounce his profligate ways.

Years later, Ignatius of Loyola depicted these two voices literally. He pictured an angel sitting on one shoulder and a devil sitting on the other. The angel always influenced for good and for God, and the devil always for evil. As this example graphically illustrates, opposing voices always seem to challenge God's call. Indeed, I believe an opposing voice often accompanies GodSpeech and in some sense authenticates it.

The Vision

We have seen how biblical characters like Peter, Paul, and Cornelius received the word of God in a vision. Through images that appeared in their minds, God spoke to them. God also uses this form of speech to address Augustine in the midst of his struggle. He has a vision of "continence" calling him to herself.

In the vision, Augustine perceives his life as free of the fleshly passions that for so long have controlled him. And this portrayal of a new life stands over against the demonic voices in his mind that have lured him away from God. Just as a perverse will has turned him away from God, the vision of a new life now entices him toward God. Through this vision, God speaks clearly to him about the change coming in his life and gives him the courage to risk obedience and trust.

Don't the words that "continence" speaks sound like Christ speaking to Augustine? If I change the speaker from "continence" to Christ, the text reads like this: "*Christ* smiled upon me with an enheartening mockery, as if to say: 'Cannot you do what these youths and these maidens do? . . . Why do you stand on yourself, and thus stand not at all? Cast yourself on *me.* Have no fear. *I* will not draw back and let you fall. Cast yourself trustfully on *me: I* will receive you and *I* will heal you.'" So clear, so powerful, and so relevant! So much like Christ. Truly, this is GodSpeech!

The Voice of Another Person

When Augustine leaves Alypius and seeks solitude in the garden under a fig tree so that he might weep alone, the intrusion comes. Kneeling there, he hears the voice of a child saying, "Take up and read. Take up and read." These simple words, apparently not directed to him, point to a new course. For a moment he considers the situation. The child has no sense of the words' purpose. Nevertheless, these words come over the garden wall into Augustine's heart and grasp him with profound conviction.

Immediately he believes that God is commanding him through the words of this child. For him, a child's speech becomes God's speech. Augustine understands the directive's specific content: he is to take up the letters of Paul and read the first passage he sees.

Twice in this narrative God speaks to Augustine through another person: first through Ponticianus and then through an unknown child. In both instances Augustine believes that God is speaking to him.

The Scriptures

Thus far I have made it clear that God historically has spoken through the texts of the Old and New Testament. Furthermore, I have urged that the words of these texts come alive through the action of the Spirit upon them or within the mind of the reader. For Augustine, the confrontation with God comes through reading the letter of Paul to the Romans.

During his visit, Ponticianus mentions Anthony's attending the church service where he heard the scriptural text that gave him a clear directive: "Go, sell what you have, give it to the poor, and you shall have treasure in heaven." This prepares Augustine to hear the words in the garden. The directive Anthony heard is a prologue to the directive Augustine hears: "Take up and read." Immediately Augustine knows what he must do. And when he picks up Paul's letters and reads that critical passage about putting away the things of this world and putting on Christ — in this moment he knows Christ is speaking to him through this text. Although the message had been written years before and addressed to another community of people, it became God's immediate address to him. As Augustine's story underscores, the text of Scripture confirms and authenticates GodSpeech.

The Convicting Presence

There is more to this event than Augustine simply reading Scripture and understanding its meaning for him and his life. The presence of God shines into his soul and dispels the darkness and gives him hope.

Until this moment he has been struggling as if the change of heart and life depends upon his own strength. But through this amazing gift of grace, he discovers that God manifests Godself to him quite apart from his self-reformation. In the power and freedom of this acceptance, he is changed and gives himself utterly to God. Grace empowers the transformation.

Before his death, Jesus promised to send his disciples a helper to be with them forever — the Holy Spirit — and Augustine is the recipient of that promise. Jesus said of the Spirit, "He will prove the world wrong about sin and righteousness and judgment: about sin, because they do not believe in me; about righteousness, because I am going to the Father and you will see me no longer; about judgment, because the ruler of this world has been condemned" (John 16:8-11).

Testimony

The God who speaks to Augustine immediately speaks through Augustine to Alypius. When Augustine tells his friend all that has happened to him, Alypius is moved to take up the Scriptures, read the next verse, and apply it to himself. Although his faith is imperfect, he wants to join Augustine on his new journey.

I think it is strangely wonderful how God speaks to one person through another. And remember — only a few hours before he gave testimony to Alypius, Augustine could not have imagined that God would speak through him.

In the narrative of Augustine's transformation we have uncovered virtually all the parts of GodSpeech that provide the substance for our understanding the syntax of GodSpeech. (The only modes absent from this narrative are those of the creation, dreams, and inward knowing, which were discussed earlier.) The syntax of GodSpeech reveals how our experiences are ordered to clarify the various disclosures of God to us.

The Syntax of an Open-Ended Narrative

Unlike Augustine, who found his peace and got a degree of closure on his quest, I now find myself listening for God to speak and endeavoring to form a distinct image in my mind of what is being said to me — that is, trying to understand the syntax of GodSpeech in my present situation. I am writing about this personal experience because I imagine there are many people who, from time to time, find themselves in a wasteland of unknowing. For me this state is not a consequence of disobedience, nor is it necessarily a time of great struggle. But it is clearly a time of deep listening and earnest seeking to diagram the sentence of my life, to get the syntax right.

A couple of years ago I retired from my position as Professor of Christian Spirituality at Columbia Theological Seminary. I was 68 years old. I had not greatly anticipated this event in my life. I have always worked, and I have loved my work. Unfortunately, I have been one of those people who has had difficulty separating my work from my play, so great was my enjoyment of my calling. So I wondered why I should retire when I liked what I was doing. But my wife's encouragement, my physical weariness, and my need for a new vision combined to persuade me that the time had come to leave the professorship at Columbia.

I retired in May, at the close of the school year. My first impulse was to take a year off to discover what retirement meant to me. That would have been a good move to make — and I did take a break during that summer. But after that I filled my calendar with appointments to teach, preach, and conduct workshops and retreats. This ploy made it possible for me to escape dealing with the meaning of this new place I had arrived at in life.

The next nine months were filled with engagements. Immediately I began to have health problems. My blood pressure would not stay down; often I got alarming readings. I added and changed medications, lost weight, and changed doctors. Still no relief. This continued until the time when, in the midst of a month-long engagement, my health forced me to come home. Visits to the doctor's office became almost as regular as mealtimes. And then came the night that I had to go to the emergency room at Emory Hospital, where I was diagnosed with congestive heart failure and immediately admitted as a patient. Over the next five days they removed gallons of fluid from my body, and I lost thirty-two pounds. My blood pressure went down immediately.

This incident was followed by a cold, then laryngitis, then shingles. By this time it had become clear to me that I needed to cancel all the engagements I had scheduled for the next six months, and I did so without regret or struggle. My health problems forced me to face my new state of affairs and myself. I asked some basic questions and began to get answers.

Who am I? Who am I when I am not a professor? When I am not traveling and speaking? As I pondered this question of identity, the thought that came to me was "I am a child of God." This identity does not depend upon my work or my travel or my being known. I believe God confirmed this essential identity.

Where am I in my life? Facing this issue lay at the heart of my resisting retirement. To retire meant that I had to acknowledge that I was approaching the end of my life. There was no new call for me, no large vision that I would devote my life to. I had lived with a demanding vision for more than fifty years. But now I was in a period that did not require a ten-year vision or even a five-year vision. In this new era, I had to learn to live in shorter spaces.

What am I to do? At first I had thought I would continue the same life that I had for the past forty years — teaching, preaching, writing, consulting, and traveling. But I wondered if God was telling me something different by "the incident," as I learned to call my experience with congestive heart failure. What was God saying to me through this?

Some years ago, when I was envisioning this place from a distance, this thought came to me: "The most important thing that I will do with you has not been done yet." I thought maybe God spoke that word to me, and I wondered what great thing I might do for God.

Several things have transpired that may be GodSpeech for me. I have been invited to be a scholar in residence at my local church; I have been invited to work with a center that is developing lay leadership; I have been asked to sit on the board of a newly formed charitable foundation; and I continue my work with three other charitable foundations. What is God saying to me through these opportunities?

Often I find myself thinking about *being* rather than *doing*. Is God speaking to me about transformation?

I have many things that I would like to write about. Others ask me to write with them or help them with their writing. Is God speaking to me in these intuitions and opportunities?

I wonder why I don't have the drive to travel and teach or preach that I had ten years ago. Is this a function of age? Is God speaking to me through my decreased desire and interest? Why am I discovering the ability to say "No"?

Along with these questions that arise out of my soul, I am becoming more interested in listening to the silent voice of creation.

I live with shorter vision. What do I expect today?

I don't feel that I have to complete a job. I can come back to it tomorrow or not at all.

After seven decades, I have a different perspective on life. Most of my life I worried about too many things for the wrong reasons.

I am not afraid of dying. Throughout my life, until recently, the thought of death had troubled me greatly. It was not dying so much as the notion of eternity that unsettled me — forever and forever and forever. But I have come to see that when I awoke to consciousness at birth, forever began for me already at that moment. Death does not change that reality.

I look forward to the next phase of being, whatever that is.

When I reflect on the things I have just written, I wonder if God is speaking to me through these changes. I wonder if God is the author of them? I even wonder if God is making my queries in these transformations a form of divine speech.

I think that what I have outlined in this chapter of my life reveals GodSpeech. It is all around me. It sounds in my ears and I hear it, but I do not fully understand it yet. I think God is speaking to me, and I pray for the courage to take the next step. Sometime in the future, at another resting place, I will look back and see more clearly what God was saying through my questions.

While the syntax of Augustine's experience seemed clear and easy to outline, much of my current experience is waiting to be diagrammed.

What is the speech of God to you today?

QUESTIONS FOR REFLECTION AND DISCUSSION
1. How is syntax used in this chapter? Illustrate your answer.
2. Why would you call what we have discussed here the syntax of GodSpeech and not mere coincidence? Or why would you argue that it *is* mere coincidence?
3. Using the parts of speech identified in Augustine's experience, how would you speak about the syntax of GodSpeech in your life today?

SUGGESTIONS FOR JOURNALING
1. Write a paragraph describing the central issue of your life today.
2. Using the categories outlined in the syntax of GodSpeech in Augustine's story, name the "parts of speech" in your life today.

CHAPTER NINE

The Practice of Listening for God

God does speak, and this divine speech both forms and transforms our world and us. Imagine what happens to those who actually hear the voice of the Spirit! The Word spoken to the unsuspecting convinces them that the human ear can indeed hear the divine voice. When this primary speech creates a new world alive with God, these individuals have been forever changed. No longer can they be satisfied with only reports about God or the repetition of confessions and creeds. They must have direct encounters with God.

Listening Postures

If you want to have these encounters, nothing is more crucial than attending to what is going on in your life. Pay attention to your thoughts, your feelings, and the events of the day. Listening to your intuitions and attending to the responses and initiatives of others also provide material for contemplation that leads to a deeper awareness of God.

Receptivity coupled with attentiveness is the key that opens us to God's disclosures. Doubtless we will not be able to hear GodSpeech in everything that occurs in a day, but being open to the possibility increases the chances that we will hear GodSpeech often. This simple openness keeps us receptive to the divine initiative when God does come to us in subtle, revealing moments. Consider how this open posture changes our relationship to our everyday lives and the manner in which we receive others.

Attending and receiving the initiatives of God invites responsiveness. Of what value are the divine disclosures if we do not respond to them? As we seriously approach this yearning, we should be aware that there are postures that best enable us to pay attention and to listen intentionally.

Ways of Intentional Listening

In my life, my becoming more deeply attentive to God was awakened and strengthened by what occurred while I was researching the history of people who had heard the voice of God. I was reading *God Calling*, the little book written by "the two listeners" that we discussed in an earlier chapter. The reading for July 13 asked, "Can you get the expectant attitude of faith? Not waiting for the next evil to befall you but awaiting with a child's joyful trust the next good in store?"[1] This question posed a new challenge for me.

At the time I read these words, I was not suffering from indifference or depression, common by-products of low expectation. Rather, I was taking every day as it came, with no particular anxiety or expectancy. I did not begin the day thinking that God might encounter me with new thoughts, experiences, or people. The question that Christ asked the two listeners — "Can you get the expectant attitude of faith?" — was also a question for me. Could I expect God to come to me in the unfolding events of each day?

As I thought about the posture of expectation, it occurred to me that expectancy is the anteroom to faith. And I found that when I intentionally began a day with an attitude of expectancy, it was much easier

1. Excerpt from *God Calling*, edited by A. J. Russell (Uhrichsville, Ohio: Barbour Publishing, Inc., 1993).

for me to see signs of the Spirit in the things I did, the people I met, and the surprises that came my way during the day.

I recall one of those days. In midmorning the phone rang. On the other end of the line I heard a voice full of despair speaking. As I listened, I heard the pain pour out, an old pain I had heard before. At the end of the conversation, I said to the caller, "I will come and see you tomorrow." The phone call, itself an intervention in my day, also invited me into the world of expectation. Toward evening of the following day, when I arrived at the home of the caller, my prayer was that I might be of help to him and his wife.

As we shared dinner together, I did a great deal of listening. I don't recall sharing any special wisdom regarding their most recent crisis. Yet, when dinner ended and I spent a few minutes in private conversation with my friend, he repeatedly affirmed his appreciation for my coming and said how much both of them felt cared for in this simple gesture. I had prayed that this might happen, but during our eating and talking together I had no special sense of God's working. But even in the absence of any profound awareness of fulfillment on my part, the Spirit was at work, and the testimony of my friend confirmed that for me. I would never have known the meaning and value of the visit otherwise. This incident shows how God can work through us even when we are essentially unaware of it. It makes me wonder: How often does God meet us during the day when we do not realize it, because nothing occurs to document the active presence?

Intentional expectancy is one listening posture that can help us meet God in the everyday. A deliberate attempt to live in the NOW, to be present to each moment of our lives, offers another posture of listening. On an average day, we are functioning on autopilot too much of the time. Automated living has dire consequences: we tune out the awareness of the simple things in our lives and plod through our days without recognizing their depth.

To live in awareness of the present plunges us more deeply into every event of our ordinary days. Instead of navigating thoughtlessly through each day, we become more sensitive to each moment. Throughout the day we can deliberately focus on what we are doing — reading the mail, greeting friends or acquaintances, eating a meal. Consider how often these simple, habitual experiences occur without our being alert to them.

My spiritual mentors have encouraged me to look upon each engagement of the day as a divine appointment. When I am able to do this, I am posturing myself to listen for God. Do I always engage my life with this heightened awareness? No. Sometimes I forget, and I live automatically. But when I awaken to my plight, I come to the present, and my sense of being changes.

"Come to the present" is in fact a directive I give myself when I realize that I am "copping out" on the moment. These four simple words have several layers of meaning for me. On one occasion they suggest, "Come to God." In another instance they call me to attend fully to what I am doing, however simple the activity. Sometimes they serve as an invitation to come home to myself. Using this rich phrase helps to maintain a listening posture.[2]

Another posture of listening involves seriously reflecting on our ideas. Every healthy mind generates a flow of images and ideas. It is busy throughout every waking hour churning out this material for consideration. This smorgasbord of mind-creations provides endless choices to focus on and to absorb into our lives. Sometimes the mind brings forth ideas that prompt anxiety and fear. Sometimes it produces images that bring us warm feelings of security and hope. The possibilities are almost limitless.

Isn't it sad that we often live in unawareness of this fertile source of GodSpeech? Perhaps if we made a point of being regularly attuned to our thoughts and wondering about them, if we frequently questioned if God was speaking to us, we might hear God in different ways. At the very least, attending our ideas and seriously reflecting on them just might help us to listen to God.

Studied reflection is still another way of listening for God. Even if we have been too preoccupied during the day to reflect on our ideas,

---

2. I have devoted an entire chapter to the idea of coming to the present in my book entitled *Living before God: Deepening Our Sense of the Divine Presence* (Grand Rapids: Eerdmans, 2000).

come to the present, or have an attitude of expectancy, we can at least review our experiences as a way of listening for God. This review can encompass a day, a month, a year, even a lifetime. Take one day, for example, and recall the various movements of your life for that twenty-four-hour period — getting up, eating breakfast, going to work, having appointments, making phone calls, meeting people, returning home, and so on. Make a list of your experiences, and one by one relive these brief periods by wondering where God was and what God may have been saying to you through each of these happenings.

Again, whether you choose a day or your lifetime for your reflection, this act of reviewing and wondering will place you in a posture to hear God in your life. If you are interested in more help with this kind of reflection, I have written about it in detail in another book.[3]

In addition to writing about this kind of reflection, I have also fully developed the notions of discerning God's presence and hearing God's call in other books.[4] Because I have explored the task of discernment in these other works, I chose not to elaborate on it again here. But I do want to introduce you to a way of listening for God that I have not written about extensively — intensive listening. I want to explore this listening posture because I believe that it holds treasures for those who will enter into its sacred field.

A Way of Intensive Listening

Intensive listening is the act of tapping into the flow of the spirit deep inside the human psyche. This way of intentional listening may be

---

3. Ben Campbell Johnson, *To Will God's Will: Beginning the Journey* (Louisville: Westminster/John Knox Press, 1987), pp. 20-33, 111-16.

4. See Ben Campbell Johnson, *Discerning God's Will* (Louisville: Westminster/John Knox Press, 1990). See also *Living before God* and *Hearing God's Call* (Grand Rapids: Eerdmans, 2002). Also helpful would be two chapters in two other books of mine: "The Practice of Discernment" in *Beyond the Ordinary* (Grand Rapids: Eerdmans, 2001) and "Discerning a Church's Mission in the Spirit" in *Imagining a Church in the Spirit* (Grand Rapids: Eerdmans, 1999).

called contemplative listening, meditational listening, or stream-of-consciousness listening. In this exercise we write down the things that come to us from our deeper layers of consciousness without judging or editing them.

Intensive listening requires an attitude of relaxed receptivity in which we clear our minds, relax our bodies, and listen to the spirit within us. To prepare for this encounter, gather paper and pens. Find a desk or a table where it is quiet and where you can sit comfortably. Relax for a few minutes, breathe deeply, and let your mind sink down into your heart. When you have become very still, you might ask, "What is going on in my life?" As you listen to the spirit within, write down the words that begin to flow from your deeper self.

As you write, let the words flow from your mind onto the paper. Write as long as words come to you. When they stop, pause, and then ask another question and write down what comes to you. Continue until you have no more questions to ask.

I believe that God often speaks to me through spontaneous writing. In fact, this way of listening and writing is a practice I've been using for a long time. In reading through some old journals that I wrote during my college years, I discovered that I often wrote prayers and then wrote the words that I thought God was speaking to me. I also frequently asked questions, and then I recorded the answers.

During this time I read the brief writings of Frank Laubach, the man who taught millions to read. In *Letters by a Modern Mystic,* Laubach described his experiences of sitting on Signal Hill and opening his mind to receive the direction of God. He would then sit down at his typewriter and put into print what he was hearing God say to him. His bold efforts gave me courage to listen more deeply and with greater discipline.

Also during my college years someone gave me a copy of *God Calling,* the little book by "the two listeners" that I have already described. Reading the words that Christ spoke to the listeners not only spoke deeply to me; it taught me more about intensive listening. So from time to time when I was searching for guidance or assurance or help, I practiced the art of listening with a pen in hand. Most of the things spoken to me were not spectacular, but generally I felt that God's speech came to me in a warm, reassuring, and nurturing manner.

Thirty years ago a friend introduced me to Ira Progoff and his work in journal workshops.[5] I ordered a copy of his book and made my way through all the journaling exercises. Progoff guided me into the depths of my soul and gave me tools to express what I was hearing through the use of an "active imagination," a subject he had studied with Carl Jung. He gave me both a framework for and a greater confidence in the act of intentional listening.

In addition to reaping the rewards of intentional listening, I did have an unusual experience of God's speaking to and through me. More than a decade ago, while I was writing another book, I kept feeling a strong urge to write down the ideas about the church that were exploding in my mind. Finally I could no longer resist this persistent pressure. So, before leaving on a trip to New York, I said, "All right, if you wish to say something to me, I will write the words on this yellow legal pad." After getting on the plane, I pulled out the pad and began to write the words that came flooding into my mind. As I listened to the words, it seemed to me that Christ was speaking to me, and I couldn't get it down quickly enough. I wrote for two hours during the flight; I wrote when I got to my hotel room; I rose early the next morning and wrote; I wrote on the flight back from my speaking engagement. Then the inspiration seemed to subside. I finished the manuscript and from time to time read it again. Each time it spoke to me. I found myself saying, "Yes," "yes," "yes" to the ideas that had come to me during those two days. Yet I was hesitant to put this manuscript into printed form. Who was I to be hearing the voice of Christ? After struggling with the material for two years and asking trusted friends to read it, I finally published the result of that listening in a booklet entitled *I Stand at the Door.* The publisher reprinted the booklet a half-dozen times over the years, and the words had a powerful impact upon those who read them. For many it seemed that God was speaking to them through the words that he had spoken to me.

5. Progoff, *At a Journal Workshop: Writing to Access the Power of the Unconscious and Evoke Creative Ability* (New York: Dialogue House, 1975).

In one of my recent books, *Living before God,* I used this method of listening to complete one of the chapters. My intent was to show others how they might listen to primary speech, but also to share the ideas that I felt God gave me. I must say that when this inspiration came to me from a deeper level of consciousness, I did not become dogmatic in my claims that it was the voice of God. I try to be open to the words that come to me. I am unwilling to say that everything I write is the word of God to me, but likewise I am unwilling to say that God is not revealed in the writing. Somewhere between this writing not being of God and being completely of God there is a middle ground. The middle ground is a dialectical relation between the sources of what is written. It is GodSpeech but it is also Ben's speech, and somewhere in that mixture there is a hint of the holy, and in reading or rereading it, God speaks.

You can discover this intensive way of listening for God by using the simple steps I outlined earlier. Although the process may seem awkward at first, stay with it and see what begins to happen in you. Listen for the God who speaks.

QUESTIONS FOR REFLECTION AND DISCUSSION
1. What is the meaning of "intensive listening"?
2. Have their been times in your life when you have felt God speaking to you? Describe one of them.

A SUGGESTION FOR JOURNALING
Set aside time to follow the instructions for intensive listening given in this chapter. Write a question in your journal and listen to the voice within that speaks. Write down everything that comes to you. Pause. Then ask another question and follow the same process.

Experiences of Intensive Listening

The Fruit of My Listening

One of the people who read this book in manuscript form asked me why I had written about all the ways that God speaks — and then filled an entire section of this book with one way of listening for God. That is a very good question! The answer is that I felt that I had written so much about discernment and shared my experiences about discernment in so many places that repetition would serve no good purpose. And it seemed to me that a number of examples of intensive listening would serve two purposes. First, these listening sessions would model fully what I am suggesting. And second, since I find inspiration in the writings, I hoped others would too. The large number of experiences that I have included here indicates the importance that I believe the practice has for the spiritual journey.

To write these reflections, I regularly set aside time to listen to the spirit within. I endeavored to hear God speak to me about the issues of my life and about the divine way of communicating with us. What you read here may only be my own deep reflections and nothing more. On the other hand, there may be "something of God" here — a word, a direction, an opening.

I suggest that you read this contemplation slowly. Listen for what God may say to you. But go further. Listen for God for yourself. Use your own spiritual ear and see what you hear.

First Words

I AM the God who speaks. Above all else, I speak to my people and show myself to them. Do not be anxious, my son. I have chosen to come to you and speak to you. The idea of GodSpeech that came into your mind years ago was not of your own making. I approached you under the cover of thought and in the hiddenness of intuition so that you would receive my guidance in the most unobtrusive way.

Though all my servants quake with awe when I come to them, it is not necessary. My presence is for good and not for evil, for the building up of my people, not for their tearing down.

I know you. You cannot do this task that you have set for yourself, but I can. I can show myself to you and help you shape the words to portray the vision. I can speak in your ear and translate the words in your heart. Yes, I am your God, and I choose to speak to you.

I have known you from all eternity, and I have known this moment of discernment would come from the day that you were conceived in my mind and from the day that you were conceived in your mother's womb. None of those who witnessed your birth would ever have suspected the intent I had for you, and even now, if they were standing before you, they would have trouble believing what I am about to do.

Do not be anxious about me; do not be anxious about others and what you imagine they are saying and thinking. It is enough for you to listen. Listen to me and write what I tell you so that it may build up my people in a time when many have ceased to believe that I speak. I will come to them and take them by the hand and lead them on the pathway of my intention and their fulfillment.

Each day I will come to you. You do not need to read books for language and images; you do not need to conjure up something to write; you do not need to strain to hear my words. These disclosures are not about words that you can imagine and write, but about me and what I choose to speak.

There is no immediate preparation that you can make. You have been preparing for this encounter all of your life. Even in your earliest days, when you did not know left from right or up from down, I was preparing you for this time. When you lived in darkness and fear, I was in the darkness with you, preparing you for this assignment. I have chosen to use all your failures and brokenness to attune your ears so that you will hear my speech and write my words.

Each day when you sit down to listen, clear your mind and your heart. Confess to me your sins, and I will forgive them. Acknowledge your fears, and I will steady you. Tell me your desires, and I will listen to you. Bring your focus to the center, and I will be there.

Calm yourself.

Be still.

Listen.

I will come to you and speak with you as friend to friend, as father to son, and as mother to daughter.

You will hear my disclosures as impulses beyond human words and speech. My revelation will come to you in the nexus between the holy and the human. My communication is deeper than words, more powerful than speech, and as profound as the human spirit. But for your sake and that of others, you must put my speech into words.

GodSpeech! It is what I intend. I will speak to you. You will speak for me.

When you sit with me, do not picture me before you. I am not an image you can see. Do not conceive of me as sitting beside you, lest you limit me. Do not think of me as behind you, overshadowing you, or walking before you, for this would make me an object or a being limited by time and space.

Think of me as Presence. I am Presence with you, in you, around you. I am Presence here, there, and everywhere. Presence liberates your mind and your imagination. Presence is personal, like nothing else you have ever known, but it is not an objective Presence. Presence is pervasive, fluid, unbounded, and intimate. It is beyond your reach, and yet Presence reaches you!

Do not ask why I called you! I will not tell you. Do not spend time

160

wondering about the why and the how and the aim of my speech to you. This is not for you to know! You may wonder, "Is it for me? Or is it for others? Or is it simply for God's glory?" Do not waste your time considering these or other possibilities. It is enough that I chose to speak and that you are willing to listen. Stet. "Let it stand."

Like every mortal that I have addressed, you wonder, "Why me?" Why did I choose you? Certainly it was not because of your gifts. I did not choose you for your family name and the history of my relationship with them. Precious few of your ancestors had any thought of me. I did not choose you because of your brilliance or your special facility with words. I did not choose you for your moral perfection or your long search for holiness. I chose you as an act of my own sovereign will. I chose you because I desired to have this relationship with you and to send a message through you. Let that be enough for you. You need know no more.

In the time ahead, when I draw you into this arena of communion, I will disclose myself to you. Perhaps you will not learn anything new, but you will learn in a new way. You will hear me speak in your innermost being, you will receive a word from me and not from others, and you will be ablaze with a profound awareness of my presence.

I will also speak to you about yourself. You have ridden your demons into the depth of your soul and conquered most. You have looked at the underbelly of your existence and light has shown into your shadow side, but you can still learn more about my way of speaking and me. You can listen both for yourself and others.

And not only will I disclose to you my ways of speaking to the believing community, but I will assure you and them how much I desire it. My voice formed the community long ago, and my people were nurtured by my Word in their midst. But from time to time they quit listening, they lose their appetite for community with me, and, perhaps worst of all, they cease expecting to hear my voice. I want people to know that I am the God who speaks.

I speak, but my friends often do not listen.

2

A Word about Being

The first word that I speak to you is "I Am." I AM. According to your grammar, "I am" is first-person present. Think about it! "I AM First Person Present." I have intentionally spoken in this double entendre. First person! Present! I AM!

This primary statement about my being defies boundary. No definition can limit it; no concept can exhaust it. I AM is inexhaustible, unbounded, and ultimately incomprehensible. Yet out of the richness of being I speak. I reveal myself.

You are in me, but you cannot find me. You have sought to prove me, not so much for myself as for yourself. Your fears that I am not present and your longing for certitude that I AM has driven you in failed efforts to penetrate the veil.

You have become aware of your own being. Because I AM, I can say, "You are." You are, and the day you became aware of it, you began to wonder where you came from. And in your imagination you traced your lineage back to the beginning, and there you wondered where you or anything else came from. Yes, you posited my being, my "AM," but there was still a chasm you could not cross. When you said to yourself, "God is," it came out with a hollow sound because your confession bounced off the veil that screens the mystery of my being from sight and touch.

On another day that you sought for proof that I AM, you looked at the stars in their orbits, you recalled the regularity of the seasons, the dependability of seedtime and harvest, and this showed you order in my creation. You reasoned that if there is order, there must be One who creates the order and sustains it. True, very true. But the distance from order to me had to cross a chasm too wide to leap. Once again your furious quest for certitude was foiled.

Ah, then you began to reflect upon your life. You viewed your life as a series of unfolding events that suggested purpose, aim, and direction. You reasoned that there is purpose in the universe, and doubtless there must be One who purposes. That logic is clear and defensible, but it still brought you to the gulf that separates the holy and the human. Not even the conviction of purpose could bridge that gap. So your quest for certitude goes on.

When following these tracks that I left in the universe failed, you turned within for the certainty that reason could not provide. Inside you found a sense of right and wrong, and with others you found that human beings have a moral consciousness. You reasoned that if all people have a conscience, there must be One who is the ground of ultimate right and wrong. You gave me that distinction, and it is true that I AM morality, I am the final good and right and just One. But this assertion did not give you certitude and did not connect you with me.

My child, you do have something of me within you that will not let you rest until you find me. You hunger for a certitude that reason cannot offer.

All your efforts do not work because the certitude that you seek cannot be grasped by reason. You must realize that you cannot define me; I am too vast for your definition. You cannot name me, for that would restrict me. Neither can you limit me with your concepts. If you could define me, if you could name me, if you could limit me, I would not be the One whom you seek. Do you not understand? I am your limit. I am your boundary. Accept it! You cannot break out of your humanness! You are shut up, corralled in the condition of finitude, and your only out must come from without.

I do not fault you for your quest. I created you with the need for certitude and the urge to pursue it. This drive speaks louder and more clearly than all the arguments that you have concocted to prove my existence. Do you not see how the result of your argument leaves you with a conviction that a god exists, but it does nothing to connect you with that god? If you pay attention to the hunger itself, if you give yourself over to the longing within you, it is more likely to lead you home. Do you see the contrast?

Perhaps it is this very contrast that is so distasteful to you. Your search for the assurance of my being places all the initiative within you; it puts you in control of the search. Attending your inner longing turns the tables. From the outset you know these longings cannot be filled by your efforts. Posturing yourself as a seeker does not satisfy you, but it prepares you.

What you long for is a Word! You wish to hear Someone call your name out of the darkness. You want to know that you are loved and valued. You yearn for a relationship with Someone who transcends space and time, destruction and decay. You hunger for something constant in the shifting values and structures of a broken society. You long for a Word.

The Word from the Beyond is so critically important because you cannot break out of the prison of finitude. Freedom must come to you. You cannot speak freedom and certitude to yourself. It must be spoken by Another. You long to hear a Word because you have learned that reason cannot fulfill you, and the god it asserts does not offer you a relationship. You, therefore, are shut up to the I AM, the God who speaks.

Now let it become clear: you do not seek me; I seek you. All your imagined seeking is but a reflex created by my search. You do not come to me; I come to you. And it is my coming that creates the possibility of a relationship. You do not grasp me; I grasp you. You have no hand large enough, no thought vast enough, no container adequate to hold me. I speak to you, and you must listen without grasping.

I see you, but you do not see me. You are always before me. I see your every move, and I know your deepest thoughts. Nothing in you escapes my concern. I am nearer to you than you are to yourself, and still you do not recognize me. I speak to you, but you do not heed because you do not know that it is I who speak.

The nexus between the human and the divine is not logic; it is love. Do you want to know me? Do you want to live in relationship with me? Do you want to know the I AM? Listen to me as I speak!

My speech has a twofold consequence. I tell you that I love you, and I invite you to love me in response. I will be known through my love for you and your love for me.

It is speech that creates the divine-human relationship, not logic. It is speech that gives you assurance of my presence, not reason. I AM. I say it again. I am First Person Present in the grammar of life. I am simple present. I am progressive present. I am future present. I am always present. Come to the present, and you will have life.

My being is so full and pervasive that you cannot capture it in a paradigm; it cannot be contained with metaphors. All analysis fails. That you cannot disprove me also adds to the validity of your quest.

Your metaphors are too weak! They are like asses with burdens too heavy to bear. A Word — that is what you have from me. It will guide you to me, if you will listen.

3

The Beginning

"In the beginning I am. . . ." The veil exists here. You cannot now nor will you ever penetrate the veil that hides my being. The child's question of where I came from can be asked but it cannot be answered. I am.

"In the beginning I said . . ." My speech broke the silence. Before I spoke, there was no sound, there was no language, and there was no relationship, because everything was in an undifferentiated unity. I was all in all.

"In the beginning I said, 'Let there be . . . ,'" and everything came into being.

By my word the cosmos came to be,
    The waters on the earth and the firmament above came to be.
By my word the living creatures came to be,
    The birds of the air, the fish of the sea, and everything that passes through the sea.
By my word you, O human, came to be,
    Made in my image, sharing my likeness, and standing as an icon of my glory.

What a glorious day it was when you came to be.

My speech was no longer empty, my words did not fade without being heard because you listened and heard me.

I spoke, and the world had being.

I spoke, and the world had order.

I spoke, and the world became populated.

I spoke, and the world flourished and grew, and reproduced.

I spoke, and the story began.

The how, the why, and the when of my creation has fascinated every creature I have made. The cosmos is my riddle, and no one knows the answer. Only I — and those to whom I show it — know its meaning.

The cosmos is a stage, and you are an actor. The drama unfolds in this generation and the next.

The cosmos is my painting exhibiting all the colors, textures, and forms that your mind can discern — and more.

The cosmos is my sculpture, an art piece to be contemplated forever.

The cosmos is a paradigm, constantly throwing off hints of my intention.

You, O man and woman, have concerned yourselves with the "how" of my creation. The answer remains hidden, but in discovering the evolving of the cosmos, some fear that the mystery is gone. The cosmos evolved out of nothing, and I am not necessary, they say. Do not concern yourself with such nonsense. Of course, I AM. It is I who spoke the world into being. Without my speech, the world would have remained in "nothingness."

Are there not myriad ways that the world could have come into being? Could I not make the world as I chose? Does it matter to you if I took a billion years or twenty-four hours? Who are you to sit in judgment of my method?

You have concerned yourself with evil in the world. You have seen the righteous suffer. You have observed good people bearing loss. You have questioned my wisdom in making a world like this one.

I will not tell you all, but I will explain one thing to you. When I created the world, I made it out of nothing. Nothing existed until I said,

"Let there be . . ." The nothing to which I spoke had the possibility of be-coming something — a world, birds and beasts, creeping things and crawling things, and human beings and their offspring. Whatever I made, I made out of nothing. When my good creation appeared, it ap-peared in the midst of nothing. This "nothing" from which creation emerged remained a counter-voice, an enemy of my original intention.

What you call evil, Satan, and the devil — this is your way of talking about this "nothing" that pervades creation. The voice of "nothing" speaks, but lacks power and persistence. This counter-voice will not si-lence my word; it cannot diminish it, and neither can it destroy it. But the counter-voice speaks in whispers and erodes the good creation.

Could I have made a different kind of world? Foolish question! This is the world that I have made, and this is the world in which I continue to speak. Listen to the Voice of Creation and not the counter-voice of ero-sion and destruction.

Does my creation amaze you? Are you sometimes shocked when you consider that there is something and not nothing? Can you see the beauty and order and purpose woven into the fabric of the creation? Stop. Look. Let yourself be amazed!

I imagined a good creation. I spoke it into being.

I imagined a creature in my own image. I formed you and protected you like a mother defends her child.

When I created you in my image, I gave you the gift of imagination. I made you bigger than yourself. You can rise above the moment and defy time. You can imagine yourself in a different place so that one space does not confine you. In the name of freedom you can take initiative that will affect my creation for good and for evil. You are free. You are re-sponsible. I have entrusted the creation to you, and I am counting on you to care for it and work toward its fulfillment.

4

Why Do You Not Listen?

My child, my creation and my image, how can I speak with you if you do not listen? How can I commune with you if you do not attend my words? You are so busy, so distracted, and so preoccupied with other gods that you cannot hear me, the source of your life.

When I initiated the grand experiment of humanity, I had hoped for communion with you. I spoke you into being. I have guided you in your development. I have lured you into consciousness. And what have you done with my gifts? You have too often attached yourself to other gods.

Why do you worship the gods who cannot speak? Why do you offer them your homage? They are not worthy of you. You can possess them and manipulate them and imagine that they will give you peace and rest, but they cannot. These gods are the works of your hands. Do you not see this? You have made them. You can control them. They are not God.

I am your God. I made you. You did not make me. You are subject to me, not I to you. Can you understand this? I speak not in anger but in pain. My voice expresses my longing for you to listen to me and engage me with your questions. How can I be your God if you do not turn to me and attend me?

Alas, it has been this way far too long. I made you, the original you. I placed you in a rich and friendly environment. I gave you a simple restriction, and this one boundary posed the great temptation. You could not admit my boundary was for your own good. You could see no reason for it. You yielded to the voice of Nothing, the erosive, corrosive power intent upon destroying my good creation.

Are you satisfied? Did you prove your humanness by crossing the line? What has your blind curiosity gained you?

It has been the same since the beginning. Every man and every woman has felt the restraint. Each has pressed against the boundary, and all have stepped across that line. Violating the boundary was not necessary, but it was inevitable.

The violation occurred not only in the first garden with your fore-bears. The violation has occurred in every garden of innocence since then. Without fail, all have stepped across the line into the darkness.

The darkness does not hide them from me. I see them always. The darkness is as the light to me. The boundary-crossers are not hidden from me, but I am hidden from them. The darkness blinds their eyes; the noise of the rebels drowns out the still, small voice. They do not hear.

Are you happy in your loneliness? Is this the life that you wish to live? I continue to call out to you. I utter my speech in Shadowland, but you do not hear me. Since that original border-crossing into the dark-ness, my relationship with you has been the same.

I am the hunter, and you are the hunted.

I am the seeker, and you are the sought-after.

I am the speaker, and you are the deaf child.

I am the forlorn lover, and you are the betrayer.

When you crossed the line into the darkness, you challenged every plan that I had for you. I wanted community, but you ran away. I wanted communion, but you became a cold, unresponsive lover. I wanted to speak with you, but your ears were stopped. What am I to do? Forget the plan? Begin anew? Sink back into despair that I made a creature who in the power of freedom has turned away from me?

I will not let you go!

I will come to you. I will call you. I will leave my memory in your heart so that you cannot rest until you listen to me.

Am I angry? Should I be?

Am I unjust?

Am I fickle?

You have ignored my speech, but you have not silenced me.

I will call out to you, and I will not let you go.

I will haunt you.

I will give you every chance to return.

5

Love Is My Name

Love is my name. I am the Lover, and you are the beloved!

I loved you long before you were a twinkle in your mother's eye. Before your mother was born, I knew you. Before your father possessed the seed of your creation, you were mine. From the foundation of the world you were in my mind. I saw you then. I knew you by name when you were yet unnamed. Your heritage is deeper than you know. Your wealth resides in me, your maker and lover.

Like a mother, I carried you in my womb. I nurtured you and gave you shape and form. When you were born, I held you in my arms and laid you naked upon my breast. I fed you with food the angels eat.

You ate. You smiled. You felt the warmth of my embrace. As the years went by, I unfolded my plan for you, a plan that was written in your being. How could I not love you?

I made you to be free. You had no compulsions that controlled you. You had no demands upon you. You stood in the fresh breezes of a New World of opportunity. You could become yourself, your very own version of humanity. I was there, cheering you on to discover your destiny. In your pursuit of authenticity and integrity, I knew that you would encounter me. I, your true lover, am at the core of your being. Surely you could not miss my presence! But you did.

How did you permit yourself to become so distracted from reality? Why did you deny the deepest impulses within your soul? You denied these deep aims that were there to guide you and attached yourself to false loves. Your big dreams and high ambitions were frustrated by false loves — the love of place, the love of position, and the love of praise. How did you fail to see that I had given you all these things before you went in mad pursuit of them?

I am a frustrated lover. I hide myself in the yearning of your heart, and you do not find me. You embrace substitutes, second-stringers, who cannot play the game. I offer you the food of angels, and you settle for fast-food snacks. Do you not feel foolish? And yet you are too embarrassed to admit that you have turned away from the Eternal Spring to drink from a broken cistern that leaks polluted water. Do not forget that there is a fountain of Living Water, fresh and clear, waiting for you!

Even though you have frustrated me with your profligacy, I have not ceased loving you. You do not experience my love because you do not recognize it. I come to you in your emptiness when your false loves fail you. Yes, I am the utter dryness cloaked in your thirst for integrity. Your parched throat and your bleary eyes are invitations to look in my direction and to drink from my Spring.

I will never stop loving you. Like a duck hen that offers her body to the fox to distract the predator from her young, I offered myself for you. Lovers do not abandon their beloved. How often must you break my heart? How many tears must I shed? How long must I wait for you to return to me, and in returning find yourself?

The shy lover cannot say it. The timid lover turns away in silence. But I am not a reluctant pursuer. I say it to your face. I shout it in the air. I want you to hear my proclamation: "I love you." I sacrifice everything for you, and nothing can stem the tide of my love for you. No unfaithfulness on your part, no lusting after other loves, no devotion to the idols of fame, success, and material gain — nothing can block my love for you. No matter how tightly you are held in the embrace of these false lovers, I am nearer to you than they. I am constantly speaking to you, whether you heed me or not.

How does it feel to be condemned to love? I love you, and you cannot do anything about it. No matter that you resist my advances, that you ignore my pleas, and that you are drawn away by the flattering words of seducers. I am shameless in my love and unembarrassed by my lack of restraint. I will not fall into despair, and I will not cease when repelled. You are my beloved, and I am here for you.

My love always invites you to come home. Home is where you belong.

My love for you reaches across all the barriers of time and space until it finds you. Whether it locates you next door or in a far country, empty and broken, it beckons you to come home. You feel it in your heart — the yearning for family, for nurture, and for acceptance.

My love stands as an open door that never closes. You do not have to knock, you do not need to put your hand on the handle, because the door is open wide for your return. Come in, come in and make this house your home, my friend.

In my house, the House of God, you have a place. The table has been set. The ample food has been prepared. The guests are arriving. And there is a place at the table for you. Do you not see your chair? Can you not read the place card with your name on it? Be seated at your Father's table and break the bread and drink the wine.

As you live in my love, I will teach you the art of loving. All the other virtues are included in love, so you need only to learn the language of love.

6

I Am Just

The words of my mouth are love, and the deeds of my hands are just.
    I love all the creatures that I have made,
    And not one of them has been forgotten.
You can see me in the face of those who suffer,
    And you can hear me in the cries of the lost.
My hand reaches out to the helpless,
    And my strength to the faint of heart.
The strong and powerful have no special place;
    They are as the weak and wandering.

When will my people learn,
    And when will they understand?

I desire not their achievements and daring feats;
    I care not for their amassing funds for spending.
My interest is not in their personal success,
    Nor in their striving for recognition.
I want them to know that I am their God,
    And they are my people.
I am their source and the fulfillment of their longing;
    I am the One to whom they owe everything.
When will they learn? When will they turn to me?

The all-powerful nations think that I do not know;
    They imagine that they and they alone can find out.
But they are deceived by their illusions.
        Where were their ears when the wall came down?
        Why did they not know?
        Were their eyes closed?
        Were their ears stopped?
        Did their hands hold useless power?
        Were their minds on war and not on peace?

I will tell you this:
    They looked but did not see.
    They listened but did not hear.
    They grasped for power, but it eluded them.
    They communicated intelligence, but it was false.
    They reeled in shock at my action.
And in all of this they did not recognize me, the Lord,
    The Creator of the universe,
        and the One before whom they live.

You are rich and have no need.
    You are blinded by your greed.
You are a wanderer on the earth.
    You have lost your way.
Do you think that I do not know?

Can you imagine that I do not see?
Will I endure your selfishness and pride forever?
    Violation of my justice I cannot abide.

While you rest in your affluence,
    I look at the helpless widow and hungry child.
I behold the jobless masses standing on street corners
    While you drive by without notice.
I hear the cry of the perishing
    Who go oft to bed without food.
I listen to the sobs of children
    With aching stomachs and parched throats.
I feel the burden of the oppressed
    Who groan beneath their loads.

I will not always hold my peace;
    My judgment will not be contained forever.
I invite you to stop and consider:
    What do you have that was not a gift?
    How can you protect your possessions from decay?
    Why do you hoard your goods when you neighbor is destitute?
    If you were weak and powerless and hungry, what would you do?
    Where will you be when the fires of justice burn?

I will await your answer.
    I will hear what you say.
I will turn neither to the right nor to the left
    Until you answer me with truth.
Speak to me, O man.
    Whisper in my ear, O woman.
What will you do when justice falls?
    How will you survive in the storm?

What? Do I not love you? Do I not care for your soul?
    I speak out of love. I judge with truth.

I wait beside you. I feel your pain.
Do not confuse my love with sentimentality!
Do not see my justice as harsh and uncaring!
Justice and love belong together.
Righteousness and peace do kiss each other!

7

The Language of God

I am the God who speaks. If you will listen, you can hear. My speech creates: it creates a world; it creates a relationship; it creates a future. I am
unlike any other god because other gods do not speak, and they have no
power. The prayer of the psalmist had it right:

Our God is in the heavens; he does whatever he pleases.

Their idols are silver and gold, the work of human hands.
They have mouths, but do not speak; eyes, but do not see.
They have ears, but do not hear; noses, but do not smell.
They have hands, but do not feel; feet, but do not walk;
they make no sound in their throats.
Those who make them are like them; so are all who trust in them (Ps.
115:3-8).
My wayward creatures form me in their own image. But it is not I
they form but their powerless substitutes, their idols.
I do not have a mouth, but I speak.
I have no eyes, but I see.
I do not have ears, but I hear.
I have no nose, but I smell.

I do not have hands, but I feel.

I have no feet, but I walk the face of the earth.

I have no throat, but I make utterances.

Is this too much for you to understand? I made you in my image. I placed my Spirit within you. I created you with a capacity to learn and know my speech. You are my only creature with the ability to speak, and because you speak, you can understand speech.

I created you in my image and placed you in a culture. In this culture you learned to speak the language of your parents. Without knowing the designation of nouns and verbs and modifiers, you were given names for things, and you were shown how things acted or were acted upon. With modifiers, these nouns and verbs became more precise and differentiated.

With these basic parts of speech you learned a grammar, and you learned how to use words in different forms to indicate past, present, and future, action received and action taken, and various states of being. By listening to the speech of those around you, you learned the syntax of the language. By ordering words in a given pattern, you could communicate with others. This marvelous gift of language gave you the tools for participating in a community.

Because I gave you both language and memory, you could create a story, a history. Not only could you recall the names of people and places and things and how these acted and interacted, but you could also recall meanings and consequences that resulted from their actions. Memory and language made you like me. Yet your finite recollection is but a miniature version of my constant awareness of what was and is and shall be.

The language of your community not only provides social intercourse; it is the language through which I speak to you. My coming to you, addressing you, and beckoning you occurs in the language you know. My reality and the depth of my speech come in a form that you can understand and remember.

But there is more to my communication than simply words. I have used the words of common speech freely in addressing you, but I have other modes of speech, not so commonly known and recognized.

I have a language, one hidden and obscure, that my friends have always wanted to learn. This mode of speaking is a ParaSpeech. It is a speech without words, and it travels around and beside the spoken words. It is communication buried in the recesses of your soul, or hidden in the events of your life, or concealed in the words of another human being speaking to you. Most often my people discern this odd speech in the sacred text of Scripture. Words written to another person or community years ago become my vehicle for speaking to people here and now.

This language, with its nouns and verbs and its grammar and syntax, differs from standard speech. Standard speech has concrete referents, but the referents of my language have the character of parable or metaphor. Direct address from me to you leaves no room for speculation. When I say, "You shall have no other gods before me," that is clear directive speech with hard boundaries. But ParaSpeech has less definition and makes room for ambiguity.

When I speak to you through other people, they may be telling you about an incident when they encountered me. But while they are telling their own story, it will seem to you that their speech is my speech to you. I say "seem" because you will not know for sure that it is directed to you. It will seem like it is, and you will be moved by it, but my speech will be shrouded in mystery. So you will take a risk when you embrace the speech.

Perhaps you wonder why I hide my communication from you in this ambiguous ParaSpeech. I have shown you repeatedly that I can confront you. I can call your name, name your sins, direct your path, and leave no room for doubt. I have spoken this way when I could not get your attention. But I desire you to search for me freely, to wonder about me, and to risk obeying me.

I am like a parent who desires the maturity of a child. If the parent makes all the decisions, gives all the directions, and saves the child from risk and uncertainty, that child will never grow up. I want you to grow up, and therefore you must learn the grammar and syntax of my speech.

There is yet another reason for this ParaSpeech. I AM, but I have no form. To form is to limit. I am Presence — eternal, abiding, nurturing, and pervasive Presence. If I always speak to you in concrete directives,

177

you will soon try to make me into an image, like the strongest authority figure in your life. When I use ParaSpeech, it is not so easy for you to attempt to shape and contain me. I am hidden, and my approach is subtle.

I want you to love me and learn my ways of speaking to you. You will find it quite an adventure if you can undertake it!

8

I Will Teach You ParaSpeech

I have spoken to you about a speech that is not contained in spoken words, a speech that is alongside of, above, or expressed within normal speech. It has no separate sounds, no special vocabulary. This ParaSpeech will often — though not always — be the meaning constructed in your mind through a slight stimulus from without. I will show you what I mean.

Yesterday when you were taking a walk, you experienced this ParaSpeech. When you turned the corner on Vine Avenue, you were moving briskly as you walked up the hill, and you did not notice the old man until you had nearly passed him. Then in a moment you caught a slight glimpse of him huddled against the brownstone wall, with his shopping cart parked on his left side and the mangy cur lying at his feet. You spoke a brief greeting to acknowledge his presence, and he responded.

All this happened in less than a second, in an instant. But then the ParaSpeech began. Do you recall how the picture of the old man with his ruddy complexion lingered in your mind? Long, gray, stringy hair framed the face you had seen. You began to imagine the pain in which he had lived and the emptiness of his life. The loneliness of living on the street with all one's belongings in a grocery cart and a cur for companionship stirred your heart. This imaginative construction of the old man's plight and deprivation occurred without effort on my part. Your sense of his privation engaged the mind my Son has been forming in you for over fifty years. His mind in you kept your attention on the poverty and pain of the old man.

Before you turned around to finish your walk and head for home, you were beginning to pick up your side of the dialogue by mentally responding with compassion. Do you remember how you thought about your blessings in the face of his need? Do you recall how your heart was moved as you thought about an old man sleeping on the street at night, cuddling with a dog to keep warm? You wondered what you should do. Then you pictured yourself stopping where the old man sat and handing him a ten-dollar bill. Your estimate of this act being a small thing was right: it was small. But it was also compassionate.

Do you see what happened in those ten minutes? You caught a glimpse of a person in need (another man who was going down to Jericho), the image of his poverty initiated a conversation in your head, and you responded by deciding to help him financially. Because you were too embarrassed to pull out a money clip that contained a hundred dollars or more, you pulled out the bill and put it in your other pocket. You were ashamed for him to see how much money you had. Then you began rehearsing your words to him. Your decision to call him "brother" was right, for he truly is your brother.

But when you got back to the spot where he had been sitting just minutes before, he was gone. Had you seen a man with a dog and a shopping cart, or did you have a vision? No, you knew that you had seen a man.

Puzzled by this turn of events, you came to the corner where you would normally turn for home — and then my speech began. You couldn't go home. You couldn't leave without at least trying to find the old man.

The pressure in your heart to stay and look for him — that came from me. I was speaking inside you without words. You responded to my words by making your way downhill to the entrance to the mall. While you were wondering how to approach the clerk in the grocery story about a man and a dog, you saw him. There he was, thirty yards in front of you, at the local pizza place. A woman was speaking warmly to him. He was smiling, and the dog, now on a leash, was wagging his tail.

You went to his side, but before you could say a word, he asked, "Will you come and eat with me?" And he put a box of fresh, hot pizza in the cart on top of all his worldly goods. The man was actually smiling as he spoke. You thought it would be an imposition if you accepted. You may have missed the most unforgettable meal of your life.

Then you told him that I had sent you. You were right about this: I did send you to the old man. I wanted you to see the deep lines in his face and the rounded shoulders that had carried a heavy load through life. And I wanted you to feel the deep longing in his heart. You said that I had sent you, and immediately he reached for the crucifix around his neck. Did you hear his words? "A blessing to you!" I knew true and immediate joy when you asked the old man to bless you, and he spoke my name: "May God bless us both."

You reached in your pocket, removed the bill, and placed it in his hands. Then you turned and left him with his pizza and his dog and his shopping cart, but you also left him with the same joy that you felt in your heart as you walked away. And you two were not the only blessed people in the mall. Remember the woman who spoke to the old man just before you arrived? When she saw your act of kindness, the joy of generosity spilled over into her heart. This joy you felt as you walked away from the scene of mercy was my concluding word to you.

This episode gave me the opportunity to teach you about Para-Speech, one of the many dialects of GodSpeech. Pay attention, and I will teach you more about my speech!

9

Instruction about My Yearning

I want you to know about visceral speech; it is the language of yearning. You know this speech; you have experienced it on many occasions. But yesterday I brought it home to you as you longed for your child. You felt the longing because you had known openness and closeness with her. She had shared the depths of her soul with you, and you had supported her in times of pain and struggle. You bonded with her in deep and meaningful ways.

But over the course of time you had to experience the breaking of that bond because she was to be bonded to another man, not to you. The dissolution of one bond and the forming of another took an unpredictable length of time because neither of you knew how to achieve it. You did not know how to let go until she claimed her freedom, and she did not know how to claim that freedom until she took a life-threatening risk.

Your daughter tried to break her bond to you, and it was painful for you and frightening for her. This double pain first came when she went her own way as an adolescent and you lost control and for a time lost communication with her. She made another effort at finding her own voice and becoming her own person by getting married. But even in that relationship she still was bound to you.

Then she tried withdrawal. She dug a canyon between the two of you. She refused even to look at you from the other side of the great divide. You thought she was angry, but she was only seeking freedom the best way she knew how. When she went away, you felt the loss. Instead of celebrating her courage to reject the old relationship with you, you were angry and pitied yourself. Months dragged on, and every attempt at conversation failed to restore the old connection.

The original relationship, now shrouded in silence, grew colder and colder. Your efforts failed. She held herself back because distancing was a prelude to the break, the final break from the grasp of your influence. Neither you nor she was prepared for what actually happened.

When you sat together one day, eating a salad, you heard words that you never expected. You felt pain for which you were unprepared. She told you that you had been a poor father, but these were not the most shocking words. You had heard these words before. You already knew that you had been absent when she needed you. You traveled and worked to build your own career while she was drowning in her self-contempt and fear. You chose your work over your home because of the pain of your marriage.

Once again you apologized for your failure at parenting. But she could not forgive you because she stood too close to the edge of the old relationship. She had to claim her freedom; she had to become her own person, separate and distinct from you. You thought the issue was your being a poor parent, and in part it was, but that was not the main issue. She was fighting for her life, struggling with her own integrity, and searching for a way to be her own person and fully married to the man with whom she had taken vows.

When you sat together at that table, you heard these words: "I don't want to be related to you anymore!" You took those words at face value. You visualized an ultimate divide between you and her, and you completely missed the struggle of soul and the pain of abandonment she was expressing. She was trying to tell you these two things, but you heard the message as all about you and not about her struggle.

She felt abandoned when as a young father you chose to work instead of spending time with her. She felt abandoned in her deepest and most personal struggle. She felt abandoned when you remarried, and she felt terrible pangs of deprivation when she saw you being more sensitive to children who were not your own flesh and blood than you had been to her. No matter how you explained your ability to be a father in a new relationship, it did not erase her emptiness; it did not fill the void in her soul. Her hunger and longing were far too deep for her to rejoice in your fulfillment; she saw the tenderness she craved being poured out upon others. Do you not understand? Do you not see the depth of deprivation and its uncontrolled reactions?

And "I don't want to be related to you" was not only a way to deal with her pain of abandonment; it was the only guard she had to keep her from falling back into the grasp of the old relationship of dependency. With the struggle raging in her soul, she played the one card that could take the trick. She made the one statement that would separate her from you and make it stick. Do you not know that when people are fighting for their lives, they say and do senseless things? Do you not realize that the struggle she was living with had greater implications for her than for you? You could not rejoice in her courage then, but maybe you can now.

Later, when you tried to talk about the incident — the "I don't want to be related to you" incident — she said, "I don't remember." If she didn't recall saying those words, how could she discuss them and make sense of them? You thought it was a lawyer's ploy, a typical response in her deposition, but maybe it was true. Maybe in the moment of speech the issues with which she was dealing were so emotion-laden that memory had wiped the words away. She doesn't remember. Must you?

And now to your yearning. You yearn for the original relationship, the one in which you are the father and she is the daughter. You hope that your relation can slip back into that old pattern and that you will feel important and valued by her. This is not to be. This cannot be. That relationship is dead. You both killed it.

Now you must go on and discover what is possible in the future. You will doubtless discover that you are in a role reversal with your firstborn. All these years you have been the parent — the one in charge, the one with strength, the one who made the decisions — but now that role will shift. As your years add up and your strength withers, she will be the parent, and you will become the child.

Perhaps this episode is but the beginning of your daughter's becoming free so that she can become truly loving and caring.

You thought that I would talk with you about my yearning for you. You were expecting a different kind of lesson in GodSpeech. You wanted to know where I am in your yearning. This is exactly what I did, if you can hear it.

IO

The Language of Yearning

Yearning is a dialect of my language. I have spoken it into your heart, and your feelings of longing and yearning are responses to my voice. Do you not see how desire expresses itself in yearning?

When I created you, I placed desire at the center of your being. The psychologists of your day and earlier eras recognized that I had hidden the seed of yearning in human hearts. They called it by many names. For one it was sexual gratification; for another, power; for still another, the desire to overcome death. But what I have placed in the human heart has more strength than all the names that have been given it.

If you reflect on your life, you will discover a myriad of ways that you have sought to satisfy this hunger. You have gratified your desires for food, clothing, shelter, and the necessities of life, and you did not silence the hunger within. You achieved financial security, and it was still there; you still hungered for something more. A sense of belonging to a community helped you, but it did not adequately satisfy the longing, either. Not even your achievements and recognition have been able to silence the hunger.

This yearning within is so great that others have sought to deny it, repress it, or expunge it from their hearts. Even Buddha's desire to be rid of desire is a manifestation of the yearning.

What is the yearning for? Is it for peace? Is it for achievement? Is it for fulfillment? You have longed for these things with the hope that each would bring the unnamed satisfaction.

The void within you and the resulting yearning to fill the void is a desire for me. It is a desire to know me, to participate in my life, and to flow in the stream of my love. No earthly attachment or achievement can fulfill you. These synthetic substitutes lack the completeness that you must have. Testing them all or plunging into the pool of hope with the determination to gorge yourself — this will not fill the void.

I, only I, am the answer to your longing.

How is this a language?

I speak my yearning for you into your soul.

Your soul answers with a yearning for me.

The yearning of the Creator and the responsive yearning of the creature create a rhythm, a reciprocal movement like a dance. I enter into you with the divine dance of desire, and you respond with yearning and searching.

Yearning is another dialect of my language, and you learn it by attending to your heart.

Have you read these words? "As a deer longs for flowing streams, so my soul longs for you, O God. My soul thirsts for God, for the living God. When shall I come and behold the face of God?" (Ps. 42:1-2).

II

My Gifts to You

I speak to you through the gifts that I have placed within you. My gifts to you are meant to be media through which I encounter you and guide you. Your gifts are distinctly yours, given by my hand. The gifts do not have a price tag on them because they are freely given. Some gifts, like your intuition and your imagination, were placed within you at your conception. They are gifts rooted in nature. But you have other gifts.

The gift of discernment is both a natural gift and a supernatural one. "Supernatural" indicates a gift imparted to you through my Spirit. When you draw upon the gift of discernment, you are drawing wisdom from me. Though this gift is from the Spirit, it can be deepened and expanded. Each time you discern the work of my Spirit in a situation or another person or even in yourself, your gift matures. Do you see how closely I am related to you through this gift?

Because the gifts are my gifts, I easily speak through them. This GiftSpeech provides me an opportunity to address you without coming face to face with you. I do not need to say "Do this" or "Do that" and thus challenge your freedom. I come to you through the gift, through the awareness and activation of your gift. It is truly I who speak to you, and my voice is hidden in your gift.

Do you see this important point? I do not desire to take away your freedom. I will not do that. I take no delight in dictating to you what you shall do or who you shall be. I delight to come to you in hiddenness, subtle and unnoticed for the most part. Only when you learn this dialect of GodSpeech will you begin to be aware that it is one of my ways of addressing you.

Does this sound too abstract? Am I making your insight more difficult? I will show you what I mean. Some months ago you were invited into a special ministry to lay men and women. You were cautious, as you should have been. At first you resisted the invitation and found ways to discourage yourself from accepting it. At the time you did not hear me in that invitation — which, of course, is one of the ways that I speak.

Your being invited into this ministry was the beginning of my speech through your gifts. You struggled with this call until it became clear that I was inviting you. Once you accepted this invitation, you began to look at the ministry through different eyes. Before, you were looking at it from the outside, as someone else's ministry. But when you were part of the ministry, you looked at it from the inside, and your vision changed.

In this situation I can show you how I speak to you through the gifts. Now that you have shifted from outside the ministry to inside it as a mentor, theologian, and consultant, your perceptions have changed. You have been brought into this ministry emotionally, and these feelings have given you a sense of intimacy that was missing before.

Now that you are in this ministry, your gifts are beginning to awaken. If you had been asked to consult with the leader prior to being brought inside, you could have, but you would have given very different guidance from the outside. Your gifts would have functioned, but in a detached way and without the energy that you now bring to this task.

Since getting inside this ministry, you feel that something is missing in it, that something needs development. This sense of need or lack or incompleteness in vision arises within you through my gift in you. You now discern rightly that the pathway is vague and the vision seems non-existent or unworkable. This perception makes you anxious and agitated. And these feelings also come from my Spirit at work in you.

You have heard me speak through your agitation over the incompleteness of the vision for this ministry. Be careful how you respond to the director. If I give you insights into the work of my Spirit, these must never be used to embarrass a servant of mine or to make yourself superior.

Pay attention to your dis-ease with the present state of the vision. Follow your intuition. Know that while you are pursuing the vision, you are genuinely pursuing me.

Continue to be open to my revelation through the gifts that I have placed within you!

12

Authorized Invitations

I have numerous ways of speaking to you, but I often speak through the lips of another person. My word comes through the prophet as proclamation, through the devout follower as affirmation, promise, direction, and illumination. My ways are innumerable, and my voice beyond your finding out.

Do you recall that on one of the journeys Paul made, his companion Barnabas invited John Mark to go along with them? I was in that invitation. I was speaking through the concern and love of Barnabas. When the fishermen left their nets, it was in response to an invitation from Jesus. I was in that invitation too. Through the years I have hidden my presence in the invitation in order to subtly reveal my intention.

You are seeking guidance for your life. You have wondered what to do in this period of retirement. Do you not imagine that I have been in your question? Have I not made this a matter of urgency for you?

In an effort to order your life and direct it toward me, you scheduled one engagement after another. Some of these engagements did not work out because of your health problems, and others faded into unimportance for you. But I have spoken to you through William with an invitation to a new work. You have been invited into a vision that is not yet clear and into a ministry that has yet to come together. Look closely at this invitation.

You have been invited to use gifts developed over a lifetime. Surely you see that this invitation draws upon insights and skills that you discovered as a young disciple. The invitation did not come through your initiative. Someone else thought of you. Someone else recognized talents in you that seemed to fit the vision that he was pursuing. Often my call comes when you have absolutely nothing to do with it.

Do you recall your reaction to this initiative of mine? When I came to you with an invitation through William, you resisted it at first. Were you reluctant because it did not pay you any money? Because you did not want to get overly committed? Because you were indifferent? Did your hesitancy stem from your lack of clarity about my voice? Perhaps each of these motives played a role in your delaying. And I prefer that you deal with my call with caution and that you respond to my voice with a degree of hesitancy. When you were younger and acted impulsively, you often made poor decisions and wasted your energy.

Think about my persistence in this present call. At first you were hesitant, but I kept speaking to you through William. He did not give up: he kept talking about your being in his circle of friends. He first placed you on the periphery, but then he brought you closer. He wanted you to be a consultant, a friend, and a co-creator of the vision. Next he wanted to consult with you by phone and visit with you in person to work through the issues related to the vision. Now he has asked you to be one of the five in the inner circle. What does this invitation say to you?

Each aspect of this interaction between you and William reveals my speech. Often I speak when there is no before and after, no buildup, and no line of cause and effect. I speak out of nothing. You do not always notice my speech, and sometimes you doubt that it is I who is speaking. Weighing options and evaluating your direction are always an important part of my call.

What I have shown you about this speech reveals my gentle, subtle, and hidden way with my people. There are some instances of clear authorization, like that of Samuel and Jeremiah and Isaiah. These encounters have been woven into the fabric of the faith story. But my more typical ways of working are less obvious. Continue to reflect on this call, and you will learn much about my "calling" speech.

13

The Confluence of Events

I speak to you in the confluence of strands of your experience in order to show you that "everything is connected to everything." No part of your life is without meaning. Though some episodes seem to be throwaway events, they are in my timing and intention a part of the whole. Therefore, you should pay attention to your life and notice what occurs daily.

I will show you what I mean. Four years ago in an offhanded conversation, you spoke to one of my servants about creating a charitable foundation that would fund ministries around the world. You had no way of knowing that your voice was my voice to him in that moment; he heard my word. In four years that foundation has been formed. This represents one strand of your life — not a major strand, but a genuine piece of your life.

Another strand of your life includes William's invitation to work with him in developing a ministry. The title you get in this work is unimportant, but it is important that you bring your gifts and insights into a ministry that is just getting off the ground. While it has the potential for much good, it is not moving swiftly, and you have the gifts to help the ministry without being noticed. In conversation with William you learned that Stanley had contributed the funding for the ministry for five years.

These two streams of your life came together at a board meeting when you sat next to Peter. In the course of conversation, Peter indicated that he knew Stanley quite well. He described Stanley in detail that made it obvious that they were more than mere acquaintances; they were good, intimate friends.

When you indicated that it would be helpful for you to know Stanley in your work with William, without hesitation Peter inquired if he could contact Stanley on your behalf. Did you notice how that happened? You did not need to pressure Peter to get this done. You did not set up the meeting, but you let things happen, and your life and ministry unfolded more clearly in that moment.

Can you not hear my voice in these events? A charitable foundation, a board meeting, a contact with a board member, and an invitation to work with a ministry that needs clearer focus and direction — all these strands of your life flowed together in a moment of time. Although you did not hear "a word" spoken to you through Peter, the confluence of several strands was nevertheless a word to you.

This "confluence of events" is my most frequent form of speech; it permits me to remain hidden in the unfolding of life, but affords me the opportunity to manifest an indication of my will. This speech is completely hidden until the moment it is heard. You could not have heard it on the day you spoke about the foundation. You did not know this meeting would occur when you agreed to work with the birthing of a new ministry. You did not force the conversation with regard to Stanley. And you did not know at first that Peter was an intimate friend of his.

Realize that I am constantly at work "in, through, with, and under" all the events of your life. Some of them are glue-like and bind things together, but others are message bearers. Last night was a message bearer to assure you of the direction of your life.

The message from last night is really quite simple. I am saying that you are on the right track, and I am going before you, opening doors and preparing the way. And I am saying that the work in which you are engaging is for the furtherance of my kingdom. I have spoken not in words but in actions.

You must learn to hear me not only in the words that I speak but also in the "words" that I do.

14

The Language of Intuition

I made you an intuitive person and thereby gave you this mode of my speech. I also speak through your senses, but I would have you learn the depth of your intuition. Intuition is the capacity to receive information from the inside, and my word often comes through it spontaneously, hidden in an image or a thought. An intuition appears in your mind with no cause-and-effect explanation. Suddenly it is there. You have received inspiration to read a book, to speak to a person, to write a word, or to change the direction of a conversation. You have experienced intuition at work when you met a new person or when you were undertaking a particular task. The intuition appears as a sudden impression of the person or a sudden insight into how to achieve the task. The suddenness and spontaneity of the idea that comes to you suggest that I have inspired it without any searching or asking on your part.

But, in addition to these spontaneous inspirations, you may also invite your intuition to answer questions and give direction. When you are facing a problem, you pose a question and listen for the inner voice to speak. When you are writing a book, you pause and wait for inspiration to write the next word. Sometimes the response to your need comes in a raging flood of ideas wrapped in emotion; at other times it is a slow trickle, drop by drop. This is intuition at work. Just the opposite of this can also happen. You have known times when your intuition fell silent and there was no water of inspiration, not even a drop.

Do you notice how I use inspiration and intuition together? Your intuition receives the inspiration of my Spirit. Inspiration means "in-breathing," and that is what I do through your intuition. I breathe into you, and thoughts and ideas flow from your intuition. Inspiration is my breath in you; it is my energy; it is my self-expression through you.

The roots of intuition reach deep into your primal consciousness. At the earlier stages, when human beings were awakening to the potentiality of mind and thought, behavior transcended understanding. In this era of development, deep impulses acted instinctively to guide "man's and woman's becoming." As consciousness differentiated and became refined, these impulses directed and informed human behavior.

I inhabit the primordial depths of the human psyche. Not every impulse and intuition comes from the stimulus of my Spirit, but some inspirations do result from my action. I choose this way to manifest myself in you because I can reside in you and work in your spiritual depths without becoming conjoined to you. I can be in you without becoming part of you. Through a thought I can speak indirectly with you in a way that does not destroy your freedom or manipulate your decisions.

I am not only in the depths of your psyche; I am in the depths of all things. In me all things have their being, their ontic rooting. Everything that exists, exists in me! And because all things inhere in me, everything affects everything! What I reveal to you through your intuition affects your life and your relationships and your choices. Your choices in turn affect the creation: through your action everything in the cosmos is affected. And because every human being has this capability, the actions of anyone affect everyone to some degree.

Those who listen to me and follow my direction bring order and creation out of chaos. Those who do not listen add to the chaos. They are agents of the "Nothing" that constantly threatens my Creation.

Speaking through your intuition always means that I come to you through indirection. This approach permits me to remain hidden, and yet it offers an avenue to have a relationship with you.

Learn the language of intuition.

15

Creation Speech

I am the God who speaks. I have always spoken. I still speak, but there are too few who listen with understanding hearts. Although my words are plain and understandable, my people do not discern them. Some have hardened their hearts and rejected my word through self-will. Others have become so used to me, speaking so routinely about me and my words, that they ignore my directives. Like children who hear their mother's admonitions to "take care of yourself," "be careful," and "remember your manners," my people have become so accustomed to my directives that they have ceased to respond to my words. My language has become routine ritual to be ignored or glossed over.

I have spoken in the creation. It is my abiding word, with all its declensions and conjugations. A faithful pray-er sang of my silent speech in the song of creation. Listen to his words, which are also my Word:

> The heavens are telling the glory of God; and the firmament proclaims his handiwork. Day to day pours forth speech, and night to night declares knowledge. There is no speech, nor are there words; their voice is not heard; yet their voice goes out through all the earth, and their words to the end of the world. In the heavens he has set a tent for the sun, which comes out like a bridegroom from his wedding canopy, and like a strong man

runs its course with joy. Its rising is from the end of the heavens, and its circuit to the end of them; and nothing is hid from its heat. (Ps. 19:1-6)

Do you understand this language? Can you look into the heavens and see my glory and majesty? Try it! Imagine making a journey into outer space, traveling at the speed of light for a thousand years. Do you feel the vastness of my reign?

Remember the wide-ranging forms of my Creation. What do they say to you? Recall the majesty of the Smoky Mountains, and the colorful beauty of the Rockies, and the sheer height and power of the Himalayas. What word do these heights speak to you?

Recall Florida's sandy beaches and their sharp contrast with the rocky, craggy beaches in Oregon and Maine. Remember the ocean view from Sagres in Portugal and the turbulent waters off Cape Town. Compare these with the warm, still waters of Paradise Beach. What do you hear from me in the changing tides, the constant rise and fall of the water, and the soft murmur of the waves? Or in the screaming voice of a gale? My word is there for the listening.

I have put my word in the seed. I have planted it in the ground, tended it with rain and sunshine, and spoken through its sprouting, growth, and fruit-bearing. Did you ever hear the word in a seed?

I utter my speech in all the cycles of life. I create in conception. I give life in birth. I nurture life through all its stages, and I involve myself with it in death!

Day after day utters my speech to a deaf and distracted world.

Will you recognize that I am speaking through every facet of nature? Nature is my language, and created things are my words, and the unfolding and interrelatedness of these creations are the syntax of my speech.

My Creation speech goes throughout the created order, to the ends of the earth. It speaks, but there is no voice. It utters its language, but there are no sounds. The ones who learn to be silent in the face of this mystery can hear my speech.

My word, like the sun, rises in the farthest corners of creation. It comes out of its tent and runs its course for the day, and there is no place to stop, for it must make its daily orbit. There is no rest for this unuttered speech. No bed has been made for it to rest from its labors.

You will do well to slow your pace and spend time in the earthly cathedral of my oratory. Listen for the vibrations within as you attend my word of creation!

16

Just Imagine

I speak with you about imagination. This faculty of the soul plays a crucial role in your hearing my speech and interpreting my language. I have created you with a faculty for speech, and the use of this faculty requires an understanding of my language. You cannot speak a language until you hear it and begin to understand it. Before you know the rules of a language — vocabulary, tenses, cases, grammar, and syntax — you must hear the language. Hearing words spoken activates your faculty for learning and speaking a language.

The way you learned your mother tongue is paradigmatic for learning my speech. To learn either your native language or GodSpeech, you must use your imagination. When you were learning to speak, your mother held a ball before you and uttered the word "ball." After dozens of repetitions, you imagined that the sound your mother made identified the object that she held in her hands.

Your first experience of naming "ball" was also an act of faith. You believed her message and connected the sounds from her mouth with the object in her hand. You made that same "ball" sound, and your mother smiled. You used her word to name the object that she had placed before you. As simple as this act may sound, it is actually a very complicated one that involves numerous stages of sound recognition and the mysterious act of uttering speech.

But when you multiply the acquisition of one word by six thousand (the number of words you could recognize when you were six years old), you have a clear picture of the enormous accomplishment. The long process of acquiring words, organizing them, and using them in a meaningful manner led to your understanding of the world. Speech became world-defining for you. Do you see the importance of speech? Do you recognize how language has formed you, and how you in turn use speech to form the world?

I refer to the complexity of language to illustrate the role of imagination in the formation of both yourself and your world because it is a model of my speech. To understand my language requires the same daring act of imagination, whether my speech arises from the external events of your life or from your inward intuitions and feelings. In both cases you engage in an act of imagination to connect experience with meaning, and in each instance the meaning is I. I am Meaning.

You learned the most basic words of my language: "God is." You may have heard the sound of those words long before they meant anything to you, but one day you heard them and took an imaginative leap from the sounds in your ears to the reality of my Being. This simple sentence created a new world for you. Repetition of it and the visions it called forth continued shaping your world.

The amplification of that simple sentence led to more complex sentences like this one: "God is great, and God is good. Let us thank him for our food." Your learning my language enlarged your world from a snapshot of reality to a wall-size painting. Your academic, social, and emotional development has multiplied the words of GodSpeech available for understanding my language.

Like learning complex sentences, understanding my speech has become more complicated. For example, you meet a person whom you respect, and she introduces you to a friend of hers, and this friend becomes your mentor for a dozen years. Through the agency of this mentor, the pathway into the future opens to you. One day it occurs to you that I have been in those proceedings, and I have directed your life, though you did not realize it at the time. But now, much later, you recognize the syntax of my speech, and you get my meaning.

Imagination also shapes the experiences of your internal world. What occurs in your emotions and intuitions requires imagination to form, name, and interpret the images in meaningful ways. Yesterday you had one of these experiences. You were pondering what I might speak with you about. In a flash you saw that both experience and imagination belong together, but you did not understand that the step from perception to naming its meaning required a daring act of imagination. You had a momentary glimpse of the importance of these components of GodSpeech, but you only fully understood it today, when I talked with you about yesterday's "intellectual vision."

You wonder what guarantees this act of imagination. What is to keep your imagination from being swept away by fantasy? What will protect it from pure delusion influenced by your self-centeredness? How will you avoid illusions of grand and noble things that have no basis in reality? These questions drive you to discern my voice, and discernment answers your queries.

Your experience of insight into imagination is but one form of the internal need for imagination. The instance I named is an indirect communication of myself to you through the use of imagination. At other times I speak directly to you. When I once said to you, "You are a servant of the Lord in waiting," there was no need for an intellectual vision, a leap of imagination. You were confronted with the truth of my voice and the reality of your situation! What I spoke needed no interpretation. You could choose to believe that it was I who was speaking, or you could decide that these words were merely the product of a hopeful imagination. At that moment you did not know that I was indeed in those words, and that in time the prophecy would come to pass. Eventually your waiting ended, and a new vision for your life was born. You are now where you are because I acted in your life, but before my action I offered you a mere glimmer of understanding. Do you see how I forecast my intention through your imagination?

Remember! Pay attention to your imagination. Let your imagination work, but do not force it or you will pervert its powers for good.

17

Mystery

My name is mystery! I have shown myself to you in creation, and you have marveled at its beauty, order, and dependability.

I have shown myself to you in moments of ecstasy when your mind went numb from overexposure to my radiance.

I have spoken in your ear words that thrill and entice you.

I have slipped the veil from my face, but still you could not see me.

You have identified my hand at work in your life and in the lives of others. You have seen my footprints as evidence that I walk before you. You have felt my breath upon your spirit as it created hunger and longing. All these brushes with me, and still such little knowledge of me.

You want to know who I am. I tell you that I am love and justice, but you cannot comprehend my word.

You long to see my face, but your eyes cannot receive my disclosure. I appear as impenetrable darkness to your mind, and my immensity paralyzes your imagination.

You reach out your hand to touch me, but I am not available for your eager grasp.

You follow my tracks, but they lead you to the river, and there the water has washed away every trace.

You ask me questions and I answer, but you do not understand my speech, and if you did understand, you still would be left in mystery.

You ask me why I made the world, and I tell you I conceived it out of love. Do you understand that motive? Is it large enough for your imagination to dance with?

You ask me what my purpose is. I tell you that I wish to be known and loved for who I am. Do you know how to respond to me?

You ask me where I came from. I tell you that "I AM." Does that satisfy you? Can you sense my presence?

Does my mystery lead you to despair of ever knowing me? Does it dampen your pursuit? Does it cripple your intention? Do not let the mystery deter you! Celebrate it even though you do not understand it.

I am mystery for your sake!

If you could see me, the light would blind you.

If you could feel me, the ecstasy would overwhelm you.

If you could embrace me, you would imagine yourself in control.

I am mystery, and the dance of delight will continue.

Listen to me, and I will tell you about the mystery of my being and the mystery of my ways with you:

I am mystery, and I hide in the darkness, darkness so thick that you cannot see.

I am mystery, and I manifest myself in the light, a light so bright that it is blinding.

I am mystery, and I speak to you, but my words are so soft that you do not hear them.

I am mystery, and I walk beside you, and my presence is so natural that you cannot believe it is I.

I am mystery, and I speak, but my language you only faintly understand. You can never become proficient in all my ways of speaking. When you have begun to learn one dialect, I speak to you in another. My dialects are as rich and varied as my nature. Not only do I speak in differing dialects; I also speak in more than one language. The words, grammar, and syntax of each language arise out of the mystery, but they also hide the mystery.

Despite all that I teach you about my speech, never think yourself a linguist of GodSpeech. You will never penetrate the mystery. You will not build a tower that can reach into the sky.

I am mystery! I always will be.

Stand! Stand in awe!

18

Friendship

I am making you aware of my language in ways that you can understand and respond to. If we are to be friends, you must learn to trust me. Through all these years I have been your friend. I have remained with you, guided and protected you, and made my presence felt. Friends do that — guide, support, and remain close.

Did I forsake you in the darkness?

Did I banish you when you divorced?

Did I ignore you in your many transitions?

Did I forget to guide you into your greatest fulfillment?

I have been your friend in all the twists and turns of your roller-coaster life.

When you were walking yesterday, the phrase "friend of God" came into your mind. Do you recall that moment? For twenty or thirty steps you thought about my friendship and what it would be like to be my friend. At that moment it did not occur to you that I was bringing this thought into your mind. This was a whisper, a slight movement in your awareness, like the gentle opening of a door. My whisper swept over you like a soft breeze within. The stimulus was strong enough to get your attention but not as strong as a direct, face-to-face word.

You may think of an experience like that as a thought, even a fleeting thought, but it is more. These gentle movements of thought in your mind arise from my whispers in your soul.

Consider the substance of my whisper. For thirty seconds yesterday you considered being my friend. You know the character of friendship — faithfulness, openness, listening, self-giving, and fulfilling. But I speak with you about another aspect of friendship: trust. At the heart of friendship is trust — one trusting another with his or her life.

Your trust stops short. You believe that I am your friend, and yet you hold me at arm's length. You are still afraid that you will experience a tragedy or supreme loss that would contradict my friendship. You secretly fear to trust me without reservation because it would open you to greater disappointment and pain. You are afraid to be intimate, afraid to give up that last vestige of reserve that you use as protection against the possibility that I may not be all-loving.

I whispered to you my friendship because I want to tell you more and to persuade you to trust me without reservation. Do you recall that I spoke to you previously about this issue? I know that you yearned to abandon yourself to me even then. You wanted the barrier to drop, but you feared I might fail you.

Listen to the confession of my servant Job: "Even though he slay me, yet will I trust in him" (Job 13:15). Do you not know that in that moment Job was tottering on the brink of despair, a despair that you have never known? He had suffered the loss of everything, even his health, and still he shouted out his trust in me. How could I betray such trust? How could I not rescue him?

What I whispered in your ear yesterday, I shout in your face today. You are my friend! Not only am I your friend; you are also my friend. But after all these years you still do not believe how valuable you are to me. You cannot imagine that I delight in you as a creation in my own image.

Drop the barriers that block me out. Give up the reserve that keeps you away from me.

For the moment, do not try to understand it. For the moment, do not struggle with what I am telling you. Be still. Bask in the awesomeness of what I say to you — that you too, like Abraham of long ago, are my friend.

Do not attend to the thought that flitted through your mind (I am too insignificant to be a friend of God) because that distracts you from the truth.

I know that you cannot remove these barriers and this resistance with your own strength. These are issues too deep for shallow remedies. But your depth is not too deep for me!

What I have asked you to do, you can do! The invitation to become my friend is accompanied by power. Nothing of value comes without struggle, and this struggle is worthy of your effort.

How can I bring you to full maturity if you do not trust me?

You will trust. I know you will because it is that time of life for you.

(Thank you. You have spoken to me at my deepest need. I feel barriers falling. I am facing my internal resistance, and I want more than anything to be your friend. Today I will trust that I am. I will live "friend of God" today.)

19

Awe

Yes! I speak to you through awe. Awe is self-awareness in reverence. Awe is the consequence of my holiness encircling your consciousness. When you become aware of my being, especially my being in relationship with your being, it creates an internal disconnect so that you experience aloneness before me. Awe is quite the opposite of ecstasy, when the soul stands outside itself and transcends the moment in sacred delight. By comparison, awe is a posture of bowed head and humble heart and looking to me in respectful waiting.

There are many types of awe-speech. I have a garden dialect in which I come to you gently and speak to you as a friend. When I make myself known to you in this way, you are not driven into utter humiliation before me; you experience me as friend. I speak your name, and you hear me. You recognize that my word is unlike other words, and the sense of awe you experience indicates the nearness of holiness. You only need to pause and acknowledge my holiness.

In addition to garden speech, there is temple speech, which sometimes comes with fire and smoke and with quaking and trembling. This awe-speech grasps you and shakes you down to your toes. When you experience my purity and power, your soul is arrested, and awe drives you into the depths of humility. You cry out, "My God! My God!"

In your humility, soul-cleansing occurs. My holiness scours away the sinfulness and scrubs off the dirt of your soul. When I have spoken awe, you have felt the cleansing of alien loves. You then answer, "Here am I, Lord. Send me."

I also speak resurrection speech, which produces an awe of splendor with radiance so bright that it blinds. I speak resurrection speech in gathered assemblies when the light of my presence shines so brightly that my people can sense my glory. You have heard this kind of awe-speech in moments of worship and praise when my presence hung like a cloud over the assembly. You felt awe when my presence seeped through in pinpoints of light and power.

Others have heard awe-speech as they journeyed down the long road of destiny. Unexpectedly and without invitation, my glory encircled them. My hand protected them. My voice spoke the dialect of awe — and they were blinded. These individuals responded with reverence, bowing down and covering their faces in humility, waiting for my direction.

Once my word has echoed off the chambers of the soul, it marks that soul forever. You may not recall the details, and you may never be able to fully express the incident in words, but you can never forget it. Like a wound, the marks made by awe remain a constant reminder of your finitude.

My presence surrounds you: holiness, power, and glory encircle you, creating the environment of your soul. Like slivers of light shining through cracks in the wall, my holiness illumines your soul. You do not know where awe comes from or where it goes, but for a holy moment it enlightens you.

The language of awe is declarative, not dialogical. You cannot speak awe to me, but I can speak awe to you. Awe comes nearest to dialogue when you bow your head and confess what is in your heart.

Awe-speech is not extended speech; it is brief. A moment of wonder, a sudden experience of deep reverence, and the speech is gone, but the memory lingers. Like the taste of a vintage wine that has a long finish, awe lingers in the soul. Like a rich, masculine perfume, its aroma settles over the soul.

Permit awe its word!

20

The Language of Embodiment

I speak the language of embodiment. I am teaching you my manner of speaking, and each way is a language or a dialect. You will never learn all the languages I speak. You will be in language school all of your life, and still you will not be fluent in all my languages. But you will learn enough to know that it is I who speak. And you will be able to discern my directions to you.

The most important and perhaps the most enduring language that I speak is embodiment. Embodiment means "in the flesh-and-blood reality of a person." I speak the person into relationships and thus into history. Embodiment defines the language of seeing so that you may observe my word. When you see my word, it takes shape in your perception and stamps itself in your memory. An authentic embodiment of GodSpeech exerts enormous power in your imagination and magnetically influences your will.

I spoke one kind of embodiment speech in the Creation, something to see, feel, hear, touch, and taste. But as you have rightly guessed, my essential embodiment came in my Son, Jesus. In Jesus I became flesh. In Jesus my word became flesh. In Jesus I spoke unblemished embodiment. Even though I spoke in Jesus with great clarity, many people still do not see my speech in him.

Jesus represents the fullness of embodiment speech, but he is not the only word of embodiment. I keep speaking through those who are united with him and bear his Spirit. And I even speak through people who do not consciously know him. I showed you an example of embodiment speech yesterday, and you received the message of love and compassion, but at first you did not recognize my speech.

The message began when you went to the baggage claim at the airport to retrieve a lost bag. The agent was polite but told you that she did not have the bag. You went to the airline's lost-and-found department, and they repeated the same message. You were persistent because the man who inadvertently picked up your bag had called you and told you that he had already deposited the bag there. All these false efforts set the stage for you to see my word in action and to experience an embodiment.

In desperation you approached a red-coat agent, but he was too busy to respond politely. Remember? Then you engaged a woman whose language was broken but whose spirit was bright. She promised you help. When she could not easily find your bag, she pointed to one of her coworkers and informed you that this person would help you.

When you followed the new source of help to another woman of slight build with a swagger in her walk, a man was at her side. At a string of bags locked together with a cable, she pointed to a black one, unlocked the cable, and the man hugged her. You wondered what was happening when he gave her his ticket envelope and she wrote something on it. I was speaking though this action, but you missed the word. You heard lust when actually it was love, my love, agape love.

Now you thought it was your turn, but there was still another person needing help in front of you. The resolute woman marched up to carousel seven, and while she was checking for this person's bags, you described your lost bag and how it had gotten lost. Before you finished, she found the other person's bag and pulled it off the carousel. But she was not too busy to say in a clear, convincing way, "I will find your bag for you."

I spoke through her actions, her feelings, and her behavior, but I was about to speak embodiment to you in an unforgettable accent. Now you and she were standing at the door of the lost baggage office. She stopped before an elderly woman who did not speak English clearly and gave her the retrieved bag and the claim check. Then in a warm, consoling voice you heard her speak to the woman: "Here is your bag. You take it and have a wonderful day." When the woman began apologizing for her inability to find the bag, the agent shushed her and touched her arm, and the distraught woman slowly walked away, pulling her bag behind her.

You saw embodiment in this agent's dealing with the frustrated man, and once again you saw embodiment in her dealing with a distraught elderly woman. Now it was your turn. With calm assurance she again promised to find your bag. Now you were beginning to experience embodiment speech. She exhausted every possibility, and still you did not have your bag. She listed options. Then she declared that she would call the man who took your bag, and she would call you with the information she found.

When you got into your car to leave without your bag, feeling the frustration of an hour of fruitless toil, you experienced contrasting speech. You picked up your cell phone and called the lost-and-found, where you had inquired about your bag just ten minutes earlier. This time, a different result. You heard the voice say, "Yes, we found your bag and mailed it to you last night." Embodiment!

Although you were already on your way home, why did you turn around and go back to the baggage-claim counter to speak with the woman who had embodied my speech to the frustrated man, the distraught woman, and you? You felt a debt of gratitude. Do you recall what she said when asked about her sensitivity and responsiveness? She said, "I like to serve people. It's who I am." She was then and is now embodiment speech.

Your return was also a dialect of embodiment!

21

Ecstasy!

Ecstasy, like awe, is another of my nonverbal modes of speech. Ecstasy is a state of consciousness in which your awareness is driven outside its normal boundaries. Ecstasy is neither irrational nor absurd nor destructive of your personhood. Ecstasy transcends the ordinary ways of knowing; it is an experience of my presence that cannot be captured with reason. Ecstasy cannot be spoken; it is felt.

Humans hunger for ecstatic experience, but they also fear it. Mystics, prophets, and saints have from time to time had visitations of my

Spirit, sometimes experiencing ecstasy without words and at other times experiencing ecstasy accompanied by words. Paul the apostle had such experiences. I elevated him to the third heaven and spoke unspeakable things to him.

There is a kinship between ecstasy and awe. In awe the holy confronts the human spirit and overcomes it with a sense of its finitude. In the presence of holiness, the human spirit is shocked into reverence; momentarily it feels its unworthiness and vulnerability. The human spirit groans its response because words seem inappropriate and weak.

Unlike intuition, ecstasy goes beyond the mere acknowledgment of an idea. In a moment of intuition, my Spirit inspires a notion that floats to the level of consciousness. Sometimes this idea is so gentle and delicate that it does not receive notice. At other times this idea has such energy that it cannot be ignored. Yet this attention can also result in its being dismissed. Ecstasy drives intuition beyond words into an expanded awareness.

Ecstasy cannot be manipulated. You can prepare for my visitation, but you cannot demand it. You may fast and pray; you may engage the silence or meditate; you may even come to your center through contemplation. But you cannot produce your own ecstasy. Ecstasy is a gift of my presence, and I choose the time of visitation.

Sometimes the experience of ecstasy is like a soft rain, a gentle spring shower that waters the soul. My Spirit gently comes like a mist and draws you out of yourself and into a momentary awareness of my immediate presence. At other times the Spirit comes like a hard rain, a thunderstorm that pours forth torrents of water without warning. The Spirit thoroughly soaks your spirit with love and power and enfolds you.

And sometimes you experience my presence in ecstasy like a stream flooded from the rains. The water rises; it rushes down the mountain to the sea; you are caught, held, and swept along by the raging waters without being able to grasp a limb from an overhanging tree. You cannot place your feet on solid ground; you are suspended and helpless in the mighty rush of my Spirit.

These ecstatic experiences may last for a moment or two, but the intensity of my presence does not depend on time. During this event you may receive insight into yourself or me, but what you receive cognitively is not as important as what you receive spiritually. Spiritually you receive a conviction that I am, and because I am, you are. You do not know more, but you know this assuredly.

The consequence of this momentary ecstatic union with me is iconic. You cannot see this change within yourself. You may not feel it deeply. But a conviction grows that I am, and that I am in you. You cannot show me to others; you can barely speak of the experience. But others will notice me. They will honor me because they see me in you. My presence functions quite unnoticeably to you; I radiate my presence to others through your ordinary actions during the day.

Do not seek ecstatic moments! Permit them, recognize them, and celebrate my presence in them. Do not be embarrassed when they come. Simply acknowledge them.

Be grateful for a deepened assurance. Then move on!

22

Silent Speech

You have already discovered that I speak in the silence. I speak without words. This is one of my favorite ways of speaking.

For me alone, wait in silence.
Be still and know that I am God!
Be still and know that I am!
Be still and know!
Be still!
Be.
B
b

23

Speech of Pain

I do not like pain. I take no delight in the suffering of my people, nor do I delight in my pain when you suffer. I am with every person who feels the sharp pain of brokenness.

I created you so that you feel the pain of a burn, the ache of a cut, and the fever-driven disorientation of an infection in your body. Pain speaks: pull your hand away from the hot stove; be more careful with the knife; take care of your body. Without pain, those simple acts of carelessness or neglect could destroy you. Pain protects.

When you experience bodily pain, it is not because I am punishing you in a vindictive way. You are often experiencing the consequences of your bad choices or pure accidents. Pay attention to your life, and you will avoid much of this pain.

But there is another kind of pain — spiritual pain, emotional pain, psychological pain. When you contradict your calling or your nature or my clearly stated intentions for humanity, you feel the inner pain of contradiction. You have the sense that you are not what you ought to be and that you are not congruent with your own being. For far too long you have not recognized my presence in feelings of ambivalence and contradiction.

Notice that when you speak ill of someone, I immediately bring this to your attention. When you violate the directives of my Spirit, you feel the disjointedness. My voice is buried in that feeling of contradiction.

What am I saying in these contradictory feelings of pain? Do you wonder about that? I am reminding you of your true self. I am calling you through the pain to turn to me. I am warning you that disaster awaits you at the end of the wrong pathway.

You should also look for my speech in times of confusion. When you do not know the pathway, when your feelings are ambivalent, when you feel alone and lost, you should know by now that I am speaking in those moments of disorientation.

The state of existential confusion helps me communicate with you because it forces you to question your ordered way of seeing. As long as you are glued into the order of reality that you have constructed, you are sealed up and closed off to my intervention. I am in your confusion. I am there, eroding your old confidence in your ordered world and opening you to a new vision.

In your physical pain, I speak healing. Your pain becomes your prayer, and I answer you.

In your emotional pain, I speak peace. Your yearning for relief connects you with my yearning for a relationship with you. I grant you peace, that you may hear my action as my word.

I speak direction to you in your confusion. Confusion is a state of being in which you are estranged from your old way and not yet committed to a new way of being in the world.

Are you perceptive? Do you see these experiences as dialogues with me — through your physical pain, through your emotional restlessness, through your lack of perception and clarity about the direction of your life?

Do not make the mistake of thinking that these experiences are "just you." They are not just your natural experiences; they are also bearers of my word and carriers of my speech.

In answer to your question about my ethics: No, I do not cause your pain so that I can speak with you. But I am in your pain, always calling you into a deeper relationship with me.

Learn to listen to your pain as one of my intended ways of speaking — not because I am angry with you but because you have become oblivious to me.

Too frequently my children seek to avoid my lessons in pain speech.

24

Whisper of Power

My language is both subtle and gentle; I speak both to you and within you. I often speak in your will. When I wish you to do a certain thing or when you wish to do a particular thing, I am present in your will to give you the strength and persistence to do it.

For a long time you have struggled with food. You have eaten too much or too little, and you have lacked control. This deficit has been an embarrassment to you for too many years. As a paradigm of my speaking in your will, consider my speech yesterday. Recall how gently but clearly my voice came to you.

Because you have been on vacation and sharing experiences with people that you love and enjoy, you have used food as a means of celebrating and a way of connecting. After several days of fine meals, good wine, and delightful company, you found your weight had gone up six pounds. Do you recall the shock you felt when you stepped on the scale? Do you recall that instant response of your spirit? You knew at a deep level that you could not afford to add more and more weight.

I was there in that moment of awareness when you recognized that to be undisciplined would lead to ill health. An instant replay of last year, when your blood pressure was out of control, added a convincing exclamation point. The energy and power of that memory echoed my voice inside you.

At that moment you decided to take control of your life and your appetite. I was in that resolve to "take control." Because I know you and your tendencies and because I love you for who you are, I clarified this intention in your mind. You decided what to do, and you began in that moment to claim your freedom from gluttony. I was there with you in that decision, giving you the power to make it and the strength to execute it.

And throughout the day you recalled that decision and lived by it. Each time you even considered revoking your decision and eating unwisely, I gave you the inner strength to resist the temptation.

You wonder if I get involved in such small things? You sometimes think that I do not care about the minutia of your everyday life. When will you learn that there is no difference in empowering you in this kind of resolve and holding the planets in their orbits? I speak the language of the tiniest urge you may feel, and I speak the cosmic language that keeps the stars in space. This breadth of passion and power exceeds your comprehension. A single grain of sand or the whole cosmos — both are alike to me!

As you review your struggle with food and the successful control of your appetite for one day, you fear that you might lose your freedom and individuality through my intervention in your life. Do not believe this lie. I respect your personhood. I gave you freedom. Why would I wish to withdraw it? Why would I make you less than human when throughout the centuries I have wanted my people to be fully human?

The language of power, which I spoke to you yesterday, is fine and subtle, but you can learn to hear it. You can benefit from it. Do not be afraid of intimacy with me. I desire your highest good.

25

Listen to the Music

I will speak to you about the language of music. You do not know too much about this dimension of divine speech, so my explanation will be simple. Perhaps as you age, you will yet learn the finer aspects of my word in music.

Music is a language. It speaks meaning from one dimension of existence to another; it brings together sound and meaning in an integrated whole. Moving from sensation to meaning crosses barriers that single-minded people often erect. The scientist listens only to the sound, and the theologian seeks only the meaning, and both miss the fullness of the message.

You often make the same mistake with my language. My language may be spoken through sight, sound, smell, taste, touch, and feelings. You must learn to hear the music and let the meaning grasp you. Do not compartmentalize my modes of speech. Keep the walls porous so that different modes of speech can interpenetrate each other.

My speech to you finds in music a pregnant analogy. Like the composer, I have something in myself that wishes to break out, to take form, and to be communicated to others so that they may share in my life with joyous abandon. With blissful energy, notes flow into the composer's mind and onto the composer's sheet until the music has been created. Once written, it lies on the page for the trained eye to read or the listening ear to hear.

Reading the music — if one can reproduce the sounds in one's head — provides an introduction to its meaning. But the full message of the composer does not come through until several things have been done. First, the instruments are selected, and the orchestra is assembled. Next come the rehearsals. Finally comes the concert itself, when the music is heard by the eager audience. The conductor calls forth the strings, then the reed instruments, and then the brass instruments to combine the sections of the orchestra into one united communication of the score.

The souls gathered in the great music hall listen to the orchestra. They are gathered up into one body as they listen to the inspiration of the composer; and, as they are drawn along measure by measure, they find themselves in a rapturous awareness of beauty and meaning. They listen to the music; they interpret the music; and they *become* the music as it possesses them and elevates them to another plane of existence.

I am the music. And I come to you in sights and sounds that embrace you and lift you into union with myself. I am the music, and you are the dance. Together we make harmony in a different key.

26

Questioned by the Master

Are you certain that you wish to learn my ways of speaking? You do realize that you cannot learn my speech unless you experience my speech, don't you? Understanding divine speech does not fall into the category of detached learning. You must hear my speech before you can learn it.

I tell you this because valiant souls have wished to learn my speech, but they did not attend classes. And in studying GodSpeech, many have found the language too difficult, and others have found my voice shattering. Do you really want to learn my ways of speaking?

You have heard my urging rightly. I have invited you — you might say chosen you — to listen to my speech. But to learn GodSpeech with its many dialects and languages will take you beyond the boundaries that your own language has established. Your native tongue has named and organized your reality; it has shielded you from the abyss. Your language has given order and structure to your experiences, but my speech will move you in new directions.

My speech dissolves boundaries; it eliminates the distance between word and reality and wipes out old sources of security. Some students have feared the loss of identity; others have come close to madness. A vision of the divine tends to blur all distinctions and give you a vision of reality that transcends language.

Can you bear to walk into the shadowland of not knowing? Can you endure a vision of the abyss? Will you trust me to hold you when you can hold onto nothing? Can you believe that I am leading you when you do not feel my touch or see my signposts?

Today, when you stand safely on the shore, you exclaim with gladness that you want to learn my ways of speech, but what will happen when you are swept out into the deep? How will you feel when you cannot touch bottom, or when you cannot see land? How will you feel when you have lost all sense of direction, and you know neither east nor west?

Can you trust me to preserve you in the sea and bring you back to land with a newfound knowledge of the depths?

You may be able to endure the depths and the disorientation, but can you endure the fire? The fire of love burns hot. It melts the hardness of your heart; it purges the impurities from your soul. While the white-hot flame sears your soul, it burns my words into it, my unrepeatable words. Those who speak with fire in their mouths do not always find eager listeners. Sometimes even good friends wonder about the sanity of the soul that has been purged in the fire. Can you bear the fire? Can you endure the flame? Will you permit the purging of the dross? Those who have learned my speech have learned it in the fire of divine love.

Can you survive the ecstasy of union and the persistence of divine presence? When I wrap your soul in the Spirit, you will know the ecstasy of joy divine that cannot be produced by human longing or artful discipline. Wrapped in the divine presence, you will know yourself as you are, you will love as you were created to love, and you will speak from another time and place.

When you have plumbed the depths and passed through the fire, you will be saturated with my presence. My Spirit will be in you in ways that you have never known before. Like a cloud, my presence will overshadow and protect you. Wherever you turn, I will be there. Whatever you think about, I will be the background. In every encounter with another, I will be the medium of relationship. You will not escape my presence! I will be in you, and you will be in me.

Now, do you really want to learn my language?

Made in the USA
Lexington, KY
28 February 2010